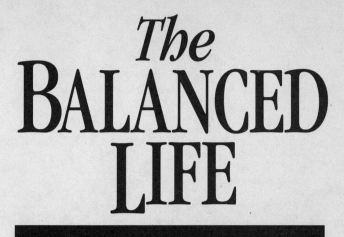

The
BALANCED
LIFE

Achieving Success in Work and Love

ALAN LOY MCGINNIS

Augsburg

MINNEAPOLIS

THE BALANCED LIFE
Achieving Success in Work and Love

Cover design by Lecy Design
Book design by Elizabeth Boyce

ISBN 0-8066-3570-3

Manufactured in the U.S.A.

C O N T E N T S

INTRODUCTION: THE QUEST FOR BALANCE

"One can live magnificently in this world, if one knows how to work and how to love, to work for the person one loves, and to love one's work."

—LEO TOLSTOY

MOST OF US WANT TO SUCCEED BOTH IN OUR CAREERS AND IN our relationships. For several years I have been studying highly successful people, asking them the secrets of their achievement. The results of these interviews with more than three hundred men and women have been surprising. I've discovered that highly effective people are not so much brilliant as balanced.

We all know obsessive workaholics who excel for a period, then burn out. By comparison, the most successful people tend to lead a "rounded" life: while they work hard on the job, they also spend time with family and friends. The question for them is not "How can I keep career and family separate?" but "How can I integrate the two?" In the long run, this approach provides more reserves of energy, greater depth of character, and a broader perspective—all attributes that contribute to success.

Finding one's balance does not come easily for anyone. In addition to my work as a family therapist, I give a talk at some corporate seminar about once a week. In both places people ask again and again, "How can I juggle a job and a family? There's never enough time for both, and my life is out of control." Today 60% of women work outside the home, including 66% of moth-

Two hundred fifty thousand women cited balancing work and family as their top concern.

ers. In a recent survey, 83% of women agreed with the statement, "Women are working out of necessity, having a hard time and nobody cares," and a government study of two hundred fifty thousand women showed "balancing work and family" was their top concern. They are trying to find an order and meaning in the complicated rhythms of their lives.

It is not a problem restricted to women. The challenge of finding a well-rounded way to live plagues men as well. I know this because of the comments I hear after speaking at business seminars. Men may fear to raise the issue in public—with their supervisors present—but in private they tell me that the combination of corporate downsizing and pressures to increase production makes for a lethal cocktail, and that a life away from the office gets harder and harder. Yankelovich Partners says half the one thousand workers it surveyed have more to do at work than two or three years ago. Forty-two percent reported spending less time with their spouses.

If a man is single, he will often tell me that he wants to marry and settle down eventually, but it looks impossible. "As it is now," he will say, "I'm constantly telling my friends that I'm unavailable because of work. How could I ever expect to have a family?"

Actually, single people on the fast-track are most at risk for losing their equilibrium, because as the old rabbis were fond of saying, "Anyone who goes too far alone goes mad." It is certainly not necessary to be married to be happy, but one must have people to love—friends, or an extended family, or a romantic relationship. (Hopefully, some of all three.) Although I will have a great deal to say about balancing career and family, I hope that if you are single, you will read "family" to mean the handful of your most important relationships.

In the current work-family discussions, many take a very bleak view of finding a resolution for these problems. For instance, a recent article in *Fortune* is entitled, "Is Your Family Wrecking Your Career (and Vice Versa)?" and the writer argues that the answer to the question is yes; if you are a devoted parent, your career will be stunted, and if you stay on the fast-track at the company, your children and your marriage will inevitably suffer. You can't have it both ways.

When presented with such a harsh choice, small wonder that some people are quitting their jobs and moving to Oregon or Vermont to try to live on a subsistence income and have "quality" time with their families.

But my research shows that such pessimism about finding a balanced way to live is unwarranted. Most of us do not want to drop out. We like our jobs and want to be stimulated by demanding situations where we can make a positive contribution. This book takes the somewhat radical position for our time that one can be a success both at work and at home, and that in fact it is the people with the best family lives and the best friendships who eventually make the best mark in their careers. The purpose of these pages, then, is to show ways to find such a healthy balance. The assumption is that certain fundamental principles of achievement will enable you both to rise in your career and to get closer to the people you care for. For Tolstoy was right: one can live magnificently if one knows how to work and how to love.

Portable Virtues

The principles we will discuss are intended to apply in our rapidly shifting world of the twenty-first century.

According to those who keep track of such things, a person starting a career today should prepare not only to change jobs frequently, but also to shift *fields* somewhere between four and eleven times. The virtues that will help us in the twenty-first century, then, must be portable. And they must have very broad application, adaptable for different situations in different fields. For just when you think you've found a well-rounded life, your career, or the place you're employed, or the town in which you live—perhaps your whole world—may suddenly change.

We will explore four laws of success, which are as old as the Bible but have very wide application. They are:

- Commitment
- Discipline
- Collaboration
- Adaptability

In the following pages, you will find two or three chapters discussing each principle, including some practical suggestions for making these laws of success regular mental habits.

From Motherhood to Management

Before turning to the formation of these virtues, I want to give an illustration of how these principles are portable and transfer back and forth between family and career. During our interviews, my colleagues and I met Marilynn Surbeck, who was supervising ten people for the Los Angeles County Bar Association. "Many of the people in my department are more intelligent than I am, and that's the way I like it," Surbeck said. "I see myself as a coalition builder. I'm here to manage and motivate these people, to keep them out of each other's hair so they can do their jobs well."

I asked how she learned these skills. "By being a parent," she replied, laughing. "As a single mother with a daughter who required lots of professional help, I had to learn fast." One of her children, now twenty-seven, has multiple physical and mental handicaps, is legally blind, and has never been able to speak. To get the best care for Holly, Surbeck has had to elicit help from many agencies, doctors, and other specialists.

"Frequently," Surbeck said, "I found myself sitting at a table in some social agency with five or six professionals, all with different ideas about what would be best for my daughter, and with their own turfs to protect. So I had to learn negotiation skills. Those people may have known more than I did about their specialties, but I knew how to bring them together and keep them on track until we found a solution. When I returned to the job market and went into management, I discovered that those were transferable skills."

How the Mental Habits for Success Are Formed

In our discussion of how certain people excel, we will break their habits down into subsets, and look at them in considerable detail. We will ask such questions as:

- What do the beliefs of successful men and women look like, and how does this inner configuration of values differ from those of people who bog down in the marshes of mediocrity?
- Does one personality type excel in business and another in love?
- What goes into the character formation of prosperous individuals?
- Where do they get so much energy?
- How do they deal with self-doubt?
- How do they plan their careers and make course corrections when those plans go awry?
- By what measurements do they determine that their schedules are getting out of alignment?

- How do they impart the principles for accomplishment to their children or to the people in their companies and clàssrooms?
- What part do their marriages play in their work, and what everyday techniques do they employ for counterbalancing career and children?

Succeeding at most enterprises is not all that complicated. As I watch many of my clients who fail to reach their goals and keep their lives centered, they are not making five hundred mistakes. They are repeating the same five or six mistakes over and over. On the other hand, as I've studied the mental habits of highly effective people, it is clear that to advance and to lead a full, well-proportioned existence, you do not need to be a candidate for Mensa. It simply requires that you make certain laws of achievement so much a part of your habitual thinking that you become brilliant at the basics.

It would be foolish to say that talent and luck will play no part in the level of success and balance we create for ourselves in the twenty-first century. Most of us will move ahead at certain intersections for no more and no less a reason than that we happened to arrive at the right place at the right time. But as John Bassler, a New York executive recruiter, told me, "If I were asked to put numbers to it, I would say that 10% of success is due to luck, 20% to intelligence and talent, and fully 70% has to do with other harder-to-define characteristics."

We can't do much about the 30%, but we can do a great deal about the 70%. And that's what we'll explore in the coming chapters.

PART ONE
COMMITMENT

1
TAPPING YOUR
INNER FIRE

"Nothing great in the world has been accomplished without passion."

—G. W. F. HEGEL

IN OUR SURVEY OF THOSE WHO SUCCEED AT BOTH THEIR careers and their relationships—and manage to keep the two in balance—we found that they were different in education, appearance, personality, and IQ. But in one area there was almost no variation. They possessed a certain passionate intensity—what my research colleagues and I came to call *commitment*. These individuals who steadily advanced knew how to give themselves to a person or a project, then continue their devotion long after the average man or woman had given up.

This does not mean that they were wild-eyed zealots or that their personalities were effusively emotional. In fact, we found a number of quiet, introverted types. But when we came to know them, we learned rather quickly that on certain issues they were quite passionate and had ardent convictions.

What are the sources of such inner fire? Some are born with less physical energy than others, and everyone must learn to pace themselves, but most of the sources of enthusiasm are psychological rather than physiological. The successful persons we interviewed seemed able to stay in the race longer, not because they were drudges possessing some native stamina. Rather, they knew how to generate an enthusiasm and energy that could propel them through the difficult stretches where the hares of the world give up.

Commitment for the Twenty-first Century

Walking across Harvard Square on a cold winter day in December 1974, twenty-one-year-old Paul Allen stopped at a kiosk and spotted the new issue of *Popular Electronics*. On the cover was a photograph of a rectangular metal machine with toggle switches and lights on the front. The headline above it screamed, "World's First Microcomputer Kit to Rival Commercial Models."

Allen bought a copy and raced back to the dorm of his friend, Bill Gates.

"I told Bill, 'Well, here's our opportunity,'" Allen recalls. For the next few days the two did little but talk. Wired from excitement and lack of sleep, they finally decided to call the Albuquerque manufacturer of this new device.

"Hello, is this Ed Roberts?" Gates asked in his high-pitched, boyish voice. Roberts acknowledged that it was. Gates said he and his friend could furnish the software to make the computer run. Roberts had heard such boasts before. "We had at least fifty people approach us saying they had a BASIC for the machine, but nobody could deliver," Roberts said later. "I told everyone, including those guys, 'Whoever shows up first with a working BASIC has the deal.'"

For the next eight weeks Allen and Gates worked virtually around the clock in the Harvard computer room, trying to do what experts at Intel said could not be done: develop a high-level computer language for the Intel 8080 chip. Gates stopped going to class and even gave up his poker games. Allen, who worked at Honeywell during the day, spent nights on the project. When they went too long without sleep, the two would pass out at the keyboard, then wake and begin typing where they had left off. Eight weeks later, they were ready, though they had not yet seen an actual Altair machine. Allen was elected to fly to Albuquerque for the demonstration, and Gates worked up to the time of Allen's flight, making last-minute fixes. If the program had even the most minute error—a single bit set wrong—it probably would not start. In Albuquerque, while Roberts and his engineers watched, Allen consulted the notes he had written on the plane for the loader program, and spent several minutes awkwardly flipping switches on the Altair's front panel. Roberts and his colleagues exchanged glances, expecting another disappointment. Allen turned on the tape reader then pressed Altair's RUN switch. For nearly fifteen minutes, tape streamed through. As the last couple of inches fed through to the take-up spindle, Allen waited expectantly.

Suddenly the Altair came to life. The teletype clacked out the words "MEMORY SIZE?" Allen entered "7K." The machine was ready for its first instruction. Allen typed "PRINT 2 + 2." The Altair teletype spat back "4."

"Those guys were really stunned to see their computer work," Allen said. "I was pretty stunned myself that it worked the first time. But I tried not to show much surprise." Shortly thereafter, Allen and Gates joined forces in Albuquerque. Their new company, Microsoft, was born in an office sandwiched between a massage parlor and an office supply store. The first employee was Chris Larson, a fellow computer nerd who had the same energy, passion, and commitment. But unfortunately Larson had to return to Seattle when the summer was over. He was a high-school sophomore.

At this writing Microsoft Corporation sucks in revenues of $8.67 billion per year, averages a stunning 25% profit, and, with no debt, keeps cash reserves of $3 billion. Both

Allen and Gates are billionaires. (Allen, who contracted Hodgkin's disease, sold out his interest in Microsoft in 1983.) At Microsoft, Gates hired people like himself: young, smart, energetic, outspoken, committed. Workers could keep their own hours and often went around barefoot, but according to Steve Wood, who became general manager in 1977, "You had to know your stuff and show it on a round-the-clock basis. We were just having fun and working really hard."

"We were just having fun and working really hard."

You may not want to emulate all of Bill Gates' habits or business tactics, but the inspired commitment such people bring to their undertakings is typical of peak performers. In a biography of Gates, Stephen Manes and Paul Andrews observe this about the founders of Microsoft: "They were beginning to realize, with an almost religious fervor, that . . . the [personal] computer would change the world." The use of the term "religious fervor" is noteworthy, because such language pops up again and again as observers try to analyze the personalities of highly effective people.

Self-motivation and commitment have always marked those who rise to the top, but in the twenty-first century it is becoming a make-or-break virtue. More and more of us will be entrepreneurs, independent contractors, and freelancers. Even when working in a large organization we will seldom have a manager on the upper floor telling us what to do or a supervisor to give us pep talks. The supervisor may be in Australia, and communication will be by email. The day of huge corporate bureaucracies and swollen government staffs—where plodding persons merely punched the clock and did what they were told—is past. People will be on their own much more and their drive must come from within.

Commitment in Romantic Love

A similar fire, leading to commitment, is to be found in all good relationships. An old college friend, who lives in Dallas, was devastated when his wife left him several years ago. He is a religious fellow, and he waited and waited for his wife to return—because of his faith, because he believed in marrying for life, and because he wanted his children to be raised by two parents. After the initial numbness wore off and his feelings started to return, the loneliness became almost unbearable, so he began to date. "At first," he told me later, "I was so unsure of myself that I assumed no attractive women would go out with an old duffer like me who really wanted to be back with his wife and kids. But as my confidence returned, I began to learn how to sort out the losers and found myself with increasingly exciting women."

Then my friend met and fell in love with a woman eight years his junior. "She was so gorgeous and so popular with guys that I didn't think I had a chance, but I couldn't stay away from her," he said. "Her two kids loved me, and before I knew it the four of us were together almost every evening. One night she told me she'd tried to resist the feelings, but that she'd fallen in love too. I made it plain that I felt an obligation to my children and to my religion to go back if possible, and that if she was willing to continue with that in mind, I'd be a very lucky fellow."

Waiting for a table at a restaurant a few weeks later, he said to her, "Dawn, I enjoy being with you so much—I don't know what I'd do now if my wife wanted me back."

"I'll never forget her reply," he says now. "She locked eyes with me and said, 'I know what *I'd* do. I'd *fight* for you.'"

It turned out that the man's wife did not return, and those two have been married eleven years. In addition to her children, now almost grown, they have a seven-year-old daughter, about whom they are crazy, and last time I visited them, they were, quite clearly, very much in love.

"I'd fight for you." Such desire for another is the most effective means a human being has for attracting and holding the opposite sex. We find it almost impossible to resist people who raise their energy when we come into the room, who obviously want to connect with us. Passion is at the heart of erotic love and it is also the key to attracting and maintaining friendships.

The psychoanalyst Rollo May calls this "generating a common field of emotion." He goes on to explain: "In everyday life, we normally tend to fall in love with those who love us. The meaning of 'wooing' and 'winning' a person is to be found here. The great 'pull' to love someone comes precisely from his or her loving you. Passion arouses an answering passion."

In later chapters we will discuss at some length the topic of sustaining motivation in both work and love, but suffice it to say here that love between a man and woman is not some illusion. It is a valid experience and a category of emotion over which we have more control than some psychologists think. We can decide when to turn up our level of energy, and the best marriages are the result of two people who resolutely commit themselves both to each other and to keeping love alive between them.

The best marriages are the result of two people who resolutely commit themselves both to each other and to keeping love alive between them.

They simply will not allow the fire to go out.

Regrettably, some people—men more than women, I'm afraid—look upon their home primarily as a place to refuel and rest for the next day's work. Small wonder that their friends or their families complain. To succeed at any enterprise requires a strong presence, so if you want a balanced life, you put some passion into interactions with the people in your house.

We can get away with spending many hours at work and still have rich friendships and a strong family as long as we apply the same commitment to the people we love as we do to our work. If you stay at the office because it is an escape from intimacy and family responsibility, that is one thing. It is another to do so because of your love for the people at home. Then the hours at work go very differently—both for you and for them. Tolstoy was right: One can live magnificently in this world if one knows how to work and how to love.

If energy is more psychological than physiological, then for the most part you have control over it. If you make a strong commitment—normally a fairly rational decision—then passion and energy begin to flow through your body.

Do Enthusiasm and Science Go Together?

"People have asked me if there are any characteristics that are common to great scientists," says David Baltimore, the Nobel laureate and head of the Whitehead Institute for Biomedical Research in Cambridge, Massachusetts. "I've thought about that quite a bit, and I'd have to say yes and no. You can be eccentric or you can be conventional. You can come to work in a tie or in a monkey suit. But if there's one thing that I believe all great scientists share, it's an obsession with science. There's no getting around it. You have to be obsessed."

The Power of Sheer Desire and Determination

The achievers of history have always known what they wanted. By that I do not mean merely that they have clear-cut goals, important as those are. This is something deeper. If these people are successful more often than others, it is largely because they *want* success more than the average person. And if they keep their lives in balance, it is because they have a fierce determination to do so.

Marilyn Monroe once wrote in her diary, "I used to think as I looked out on the Hollywood night, *There must be thousands of girls sitting alone like me, dreaming of becoming a movie star. But I'm not going to worry about them. I'm dreaming the hardest.*" There can be no question that such motivation, in addition to her natural sexual allure, helped catapult Monroe to stardom.

> "Winning is not everything. But wanting *to win is.*"
> —Vince Lombardi

Every coach has a locker full of stories about good athletes who eventually washed out because they had insufficient fire in the belly. They may have been blessed with an abundance of talent, but accompanying it they had no taste for the blood and sweat necessary to become a winner.

Abraham Lincoln, responding to a young man who asked advice about studying law, wrote something similar: "If you are resolutely determined to make a lawyer of yourself, the thing is more than half done already. Always bear in mind that your resolution to succeed is more important than any other thing."

Lincoln exemplified the fervent commitment he encouraged in others. A few biographers mistakenly depict Lincoln as the mild, moderate, ever-forgiving president who compromised whenever necessary to keep people mollified. He may have been patient and compassionate, but there was nothing tepid in his temperament. In the depths of the Civil

War, when it seemed as if the slaughter would never end, Lincoln's ardent devotion to the Union and later to emancipation galvanized the will of the country. This fire was detectable quite early in his speeches. As a young man, he lacked many of the natural qualities of the orator—his appearance was ungainly, his voice high pitched, his style of gesturing awkward. What he had was dedication. A Springfield man in one of Lincoln's audiences gave this picture: "As his body loosened and swayed to the cadence of his address and as his thoughts unfolded, drops of sweat stood out on his forehead; he was speaking not only with his tongue but with every blood drop of his body." Another observer said: "His manner was impassioned and he seemed transfigured; his listeners felt that he believed every word he said and that like Martin Luther he would go to the stake rather than abate one jot or tittle of it."

Such conviction is typical of people who gain great stature. They have firm credos and carry with them strongly held beliefs. They stand for certain things, regardless of how many people are turning tail and running. How did Jesus elicit such loyalty and such achievement from his ragtag band of disciples? And how is it that he still electrifies young people today? There are many reasons, but one of the primary ones is that he conveyed a passionate ardor and summoned his followers to a life of similar personal power. When forces such as Jesus stride across the scene, they are never lukewarm, and no one has ever been able to ignore the power of such committed believers.

The Remarkable Man from Arkansas

If we need further evidence that liberality of desire can lead to remarkable success, the story of Samuel Moore Walton will help. A short, wiry fellow who grew up during the Depression in the small towns of Oklahoma and Missouri, he did well enough in school ("I wasn't what you'd call a gifted student," he wrote, "but I worked really hard and made the honor roll"), saved $5,000 while in the Army and used it to buy a dog of a variety store in Newport, Arkansas. The building was fifty by one hundred feet and looked out onto the railroad tracks. Within five years Walton had turned the store from a money loser into a profitable venture. But he had been naive about contracts, and the landlord, smelling an opportunity, refused to renew the lease and put his son into the building. So Walton had to begin all over again in a different city.

Forty years later, Walton's company, now called Wal-Mart, owned 1,528 stores, and *Forbes* magazine named him the richest person in America. Writing about all this, Walton said: "I think I overcame every single one of my personal shortcomings by the sheer passion I brought to my work. I don't know if you're born with that kind of passion, or if you can learn it. But I do know you need it. If you love your work, you'll be out there every day trying to do it the best you possibly can, and pretty soon everybody around will catch the passion from you—like a fever."

Walton's commitment manifested itself in his family as much as in his career. Here is what his daughter Alice said about their yearly four-week vacations: "We would get in the station wagon—four kids and the dog—strap the canoe on top and hitch up a home-made trailer behind, and take off for a different part of the country every summer. We would always do it as long as Dad could stop and see stores along the way." Asked about Walton's "workaholic" hours, Alice replied, "It's interesting. I know Dad worked incredible hours, and I know he traveled a lot, but I never felt like he was gone much. He went out of his way to spend time with us, and he was fun to be with. He loved to play baseball with us. I tagged along with him on his trips a good bit, and I still visit stores because of it."

Why Some People Accomplish
So Much in a Lifetime

For several years I have scratched my head over the phenomenon of people like Sam Walton, who describe themselves as "ordinary." Why do certain average people
eventually rise to so much higher a level, both in work and
in relationships, than their more brilliant counterparts? The
trajectory of the brilliant failure looks like this:

Figure 1: The Brilliant Failure

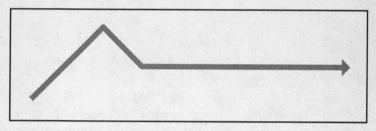

These people are bright, popular, have a great deal of
talent, and at first seem to have the thrust of a Saturn rocket.
Everyone recognizes their gifts in school. They are the
beauty queens, the star athletes, the people who get dates
easily. Perhaps they are voted "Most Likely to Succeed,"
and indeed they do well at first. But then at some point they
stumble. Perhaps they have a failure like Walton's first
store, or lose a job for the first time. Perhaps they go
through a divorce or start a business that ends in bankruptcy. Perhaps there is some scandal. In any case, the
reversal is such a shock and so painful that the remainder of
their lives is spent fearing it will happen again. They retract,
become more conservative. They fear ever to dream
grandly again or to commit themselves fully to another person again. And eventually they fizzle like a wet firecracker.

On the other hand, most of us have also known people
like Walton, who were not fast-trackers, who did not begin

with a meteoric rise, but who continued to move upward:

Figure 2: The Ordinary Achiever Who Rises Slowly But Eventually Succeeds

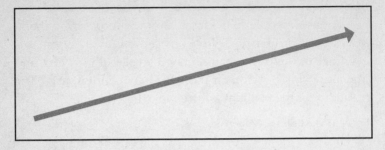

For these "average" men and women, gradual, steady progress pays off and ultimately they accomplish far more than those who began with such a flourish.

But as we examine the above diagram, it is still not an accurate depiction of how people get ahead, for progress never occurs in such a steady line, moving unremittingly upward. Progress happens by fits and starts, zigzagging upward, with many reverses. Effective, balanced people expect failures and changes in the terrain, and although they usually have severe difficulties, they are not thrown by these detours. Their path looks more like this:

Figure 3: The Achiever Who Has Learned to Adapt to Change and Failure

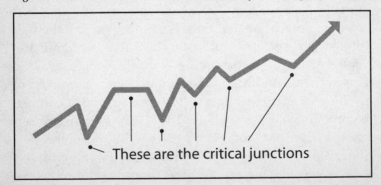

These are the critical junctions

What is it that keeps these successful men and women moving through the ups and downs of change and setback? It is their commitment. They possess a fire to reach certain goals. When circumstances turn against them or when they fail, this passion triggers even more energy. Their commitment enables them to bounce back.

The Dark Side of Passion

This is not to say that all passion is good. The effective men and women we are examining are not wild-eyed egomaniacs, crash dieters, religious fanatics, or members of hate groups. Fervor run amuck is the most destructive of forces. Hence the seers have warned that desire without reason will lead to chaos and that powerful emotions must be channeled and held in check by compassion.

Fanatics and zealots usually have a glint of hostility flashing in their eyes and are like forest fires burning brightly but destroying everything in their path that is green and tender. Healthy men and women of passion, on the other hand, are often distinguished by the ardor with which they love. They can be obsessive about their goals and a little hard on people who get in their way, but their ultimate objective is to build rather than to destroy. The value of passion, like the value of fire, is judged finally by the amount of warmth and light it creates.

Whatever the problems caused by passion, it is the necessary force needed for peak performance. A former sales manager for NCR once said: "Genius is intensity. The salesman who surges with enthusiasm, though it is excessive, is superior to the one who has no passion. I would prefer to calm down a geyser than start with a mud hole."

2

FOCUS: DOING A FEW THINGS WELL

"Put yourself wholeheartedly into something, and energy grows. It seems inexhaustible. If, on the other hand, you are divided and conflicted about what you are doing, you create anxiety. And the amount of physical and emotional energy consumed by anxiety is exorbitant."

—HELEN DE ROSI, M. D.

WHEN GEORGE GALLUP, JR. POLLED A GROUP OF PEOPLE WHO had achieved enough to be listed in *Who's Who*, he asked them to rate the abilities they considered most important for their success. The respondents were quite modest about their intelligence. Most did not rate themselves in the top category for IQ. But three-fourths rated themselves in the top percentiles when asked about "becoming a master in some field."

The passionate desire we discussed in the last chapter is the trigger for commitment, but if you are to lead a committed life, it will require more than emotional intensity. Among other things, you must develop an ability to channel your energy, to focus on only the important pursuits. No airplane reaches its destination unless it is kept on course, no steam drives a turbine unless it is confined, no river produces electricity until it is tunneled, no life grows great until it is focused. All balanced people know this principle of singleness, of concentration, of keeping your eye on the ball.

The Steps to Mastery

The steps in attaining focus, and the high level of competency that accompanies focus, are rather simple:
1. Find a specialty for which you are gifted.
2. Select work you love.
3. Strip away nonessential demands on your time until your schedule reflects your scale of values.
4. Strengthen your powers of concentration.

We will look first at how focus leads to mastery in one's career, then turn to the question of whether people who are intensely committed to their careers can also have good relationships.

Step 1. Find a specialty for which you are gifted.

The first step on the road to mastery is to identify your gifts. In part this includes facing the fact that you can't be good at everything. "Some people exercise incredibly poor career management," says Rex Shannon, the former CEO at Fidelity Union Insurance in Dallas. "They are floundering because they're in a field for which they have absolutely no talent, and which they will grow to hate. If they exercised a little courage and moved into a job where they had aptitude—even if it meant a cut in pay at first—they could quickly succeed."

When I talk to my patients about identifying their gifts, they often respond, "But, Dr. McGinnis, you don't understand. I'm not good at *any*thing." I worry about such people, because evidently they have been battered by some tough rejections. If you have been cut from athletic teams, eliminated from debate contests, terminated from jobs, told by various authorities that you were not good enough, it is difficult to believe you have something unique to offer the world. However, it is my stubborn notion that we all (including those of us who are emotionally ill or mentally disabled) have some particularity, some interest we can turn into a specialty, some craft at which we can excel.

Building on Success. Although the sorting can be difficult, and some false starts are inevitable, once we have found a specialty, we can move on to bigger achievements by parlaying our early successes. Thomas Watson, Jr. tells of the difficulties he had living in the shadow of his father, the founder of IBM. Young Watson was a lackluster student, showed little promise in either high school or college, and even required a tutor to get through the IBM sales school.

But when Watson took flying lessons, something suddenly took hold. "What a feeling!" he writes. "I was good at flying, instantly good. I plowed everything I could, mentally, physically, and financially into this mad pursuit, and gained a lot of self-confidence."

This single achievement led to other accomplishments. Because of his experience as a pilot, Watson quickly became an officer in the Air Force during World War II. "Those years were the most important ones in my life," he says, "because there I found that though I was not brilliant, I had an orderly mind and an unusual ability to focus on what was important and put it across to others." Watson eventually went on to become president of IBM, and dragged the company, kicking and screaming, into the computer age. In fifteen years he and his colleagues increased revenues at IBM from $743 million to $7.5 billion, a tenfold gain.

It is startling how many persons of accomplishment have had such early experiences of rejection and failure. Disappointment in one area seems to have motivated them to excel in another. It is the law of compensation. Rather than becoming

Rather than becoming obsessed with their weaknesses, they compensate by developing their strengths.

obsessed with their weaknesses, they compensate by developing their strengths. They keep experimenting until they find something where they have aptitude, then make that proficiency the foundation for further achievements. The psychological law here is that the more we dwell on our weaknesses, the weaker we become; and the more we develop our strengths, the more personal power we find.

R_x for Parenting: Help Your Child Become Good in at Least One Field

Child psychologist and founder of Focus on the Family, Dr. James Dobson, suggests that parents help their children become as good as they possibly can be in at least one area. If it's not football, maybe it will be basketball. If they're not athletic, help them excel musically or in some academic subject.

When Dobson was a small boy, his father took him out to the tennis court one Saturday morning with a bucket of balls and began to teach him tennis. "That was a regular Saturday ritual," he says. "And some Saturdays, I didn't want to go out and hit another hundred balls, but I'm very glad that my father spotted some talent in me, then kept his thumb in my back. Because when I was in junior high, I was a very shy, skinny kid, not at all sure of myself. But if I had been asked to write an essay about what I liked about myself, the one thing I could have said was 'I'm the best tennis player in the seventh grade.'"

It is an excellent model for childrearing and an excellent model for achieving excellence in our adult lives.

The question then becomes "How am I smart?" rather than "How smart am I?" Howard Gardner, a psychologist at Harvard, has been saying for many years that the human mind contains far more types of intelligence than can be measured with a paper-and-pencil test in schools. Standard IQ tests measure only two kinds of ability—math and language skills. But according to Gardner we have at least seven basic abilities or skills: mathematical/logical, linguistic, musical, spatial, bodily/kinesthetic, and two types of personal intelligence that might be described as interpersonal and intrapersonal (how you deal with others and how you deal with your inner self).

In looking at some of the titans of history, Gardner discovered that while they were talented in certain areas, they had glaring gaps in others:

- Sigmund Freud, for instance, lacked any musical and spatial abilities, but he used his linguistic and intrapersonal skills to become the founder of modern psychology.
- Albert Einstein, on the other hand, had scant personal insights. His gifts were logical-spatial and he concentrated there.
- Poor at academics, Pablo Picasso loved spatial and psychomotor pursuits and they enabled him to become a fabled painter.
- T. S. Eliot had musical limitations and few bodily skills, but was strong in linguistics and scholastics and he exercised those gifts in his poetry.
- Martha Graham had no aptitude in the logical-mathematical arena, but brilliant in kinetics, she became a great dancer.
- Gandhi lacked artistic keenness—his talents were personal and linguistic. He became a religious giant and led India to independence.

As they were beginning their careers, it would have been easy for any of these people to become obsessed with their weaknesses. Fortunately, they capitalized on their strengths instead.

Normally, we will not find it hard to identify the places where we have interests and strengths. A woman said recently, "Everyone has talent. What is rare is the courage to follow that talent to the place where it leads." The

> "Sometimes you have to play a long time to play like yourself."
> —Miles Davis

key is to submit to the hard work of polishing our gifts until we become the best in the field that we can possibly be.

Step 2. Select work you love.

You don't have to be a workaholic to become successful, but it helps if you enjoy what you do and are able to follow the injunction from Ecclesiastes 9:10, "Whatever your hand finds to do, do with your might." Robin Burns, forty-three, has come a long way since her childhood in Cripple Creek, Colorado. She is president and CEO of the Estèe Lauder USA Cosmetics Company, and at an estimated salary of $1.5 million a year, is one of the nation's best-paid women executives. Since school, Burns has held three positions and "loved them all." When a reporter asked about the dozen part-time jobs that helped put Burns through school, she used the same word. She "loved" them too.

When one encounters a person such as Burns, it is obvious that she not only has found jobs she likes, but that she also takes a high view of work itself. Finding herself in the midst of a given task, she determines both to give herself to that task with total dedication and to deliberately have fun while doing it.

Consider a man who has not moved in the prestigious echelons occupied by people like Burns, and who makes far less money than the head of IBM. When Luis Hernandez escaped from Cuba in 1970, his license as a pharmacist was not valid in the United States, so he had to take a job as an assistant church custodian in Glendale, California. He enjoyed the physical labor and grew to like the parishioners so much that he decided he had found a job he could enjoy for the rest of his life. He soon rose to become head custodian, but since he needed the extra income, he also continued to do the assistant's work. Gradually learning the best cleaners and waxes, Hernandez persuaded the church to buy good equipment, and he improved his procedures until the buildings glistened.

Unlike some custodians—who become crotchety with people and whose goal is to limit usage of their buildings in order to keep their work at a minimum—Hernandez saw the parishioners as his customers and went to great lengths to make it possible for the facilities to get full use. He was happy that the church rooms were busy because he believed much good came from the meetings there.

For almost thirty years Hernandez has cheerfully done a two-person job and seems thoroughly fulfilled caring for the house of God. He is so appreciated by hundreds of people in the congregation that they pay him quite well. How has this man made such a success of his job? By selecting work he can do well, finding ways to be the best custodian he can be, and by turning his job into a cause. He has focused his life and achieved a high state of energy and excellence, in large part because he loves his work.

According to one study of millionaires, an impressive majority eventually became wealthy not because they possessed a primary ambition to get rich, but because they found work about which they could be passionate. Their "luck" arose from their dedication to an area they enjoyed. The universe bends to those who are convinced that they are in the right place doing the right thing, and when average people become zealous about the task before them, they are no longer average.

The patient sitting before me had come to our clinic with stress that gave him lower back pain, headaches, and constant diarrhea. His doctor could find no medical cause for any of these symptoms and suggested that he see a psychotherapist. As we analyzed the various sections of his life, I learned that he had a fine family and never had the stress symptoms on the weekends—no matter how strenuous his activities. So it didn't take a brilliant therapist to decide to concentrate on his work. I learned that as an engineer, he had been moderately happy, and because he worked hard, he had been promoted to supervising a group of other engineers, a job he found to be quite disagreeable. To make matters worse, his boss's management style was to browbeat subordinates all day long. Small wonder that my client's stomach would not work Monday through Friday.

Could he go back to being an engineer or take his management skills to another company? I wondered aloud. No, he was sick of the entire industry, and the more we talked, the clearer it became that he wanted out. In our sessions we explored the occasions when he had felt most fulfilled, and it turned out that he was happiest on weekends, building furniture in his garage amid the smell of wood shavings and lacquer thinner. It took some courage to make the switch, but he has operated his own cabinet shop now for almost ten years, works with two apprentices, and is widely known for the quality of his pieces. He may or may not get rich, but he has found something he enjoys, has learned to do it well, and for the first time in his life whistles while he works.

Step 3. Strip away nonessential demands on your time until your schedule reflects your scale of values.

If you are focused, you are willing to say no to many demands and prune your activities in order to devote yourself fully to the most important endeavors. Jesus speaks with great wisdom about focus. In a set of three parables, the best known of which is the parable of the pearl of great price, he holds up as an example the people who give all they have to achieve one great thing.

Balanced people have a fire to reach certain objectives, but they usually set fewer goals than their counterparts. Then, when they do set an objective, they make whatever sacrifices are necessary and hang on until it is accomplished.

The brilliant failures of this world are very different. The problem often is not laziness—they sometimes lead active lives and summon lots of passion for their projects— it is tenacity that is missing. Their passion gets dissipated with the result that they are divided rather than integrated. Dabbling in everything, they fail to become extraordinarily good at anything.

This dissipation of one's days is seldom intentional. In fact, it is largely unconscious. The first step, then, is to bring to consciousness the question of objectives, and to list (doing so with pen and paper is helpful) the people and projects that are significant to you. The next step is to rank the goals. With such ordering it becomes fairly easy to strip away unnecessary expenditures of time. You no longer allow yourself to be distracted by demands that cry "urgent" when goals lie quietly before you that are actually more important.

Dianna Booher, in her book *Get a Life Without Sacrificing Your Career*, makes this analysis: "Long-term, high-priority activities never seem urgent. We delay in doing the most important things because the payoff will come so much later." Booher goes on to make this practical suggestion: "If you have difficulty getting No out of your mouth when someone seems to have a good cause, think of the No in a positive way. Think of the No to one thing as a Yes to something else. Instead of saying, 'No, I can't do X,' try, 'I've decided to devote all my time and attention to Y.' Focus the conversation on what you have decided to commit to rather than on what you have decided not to commit to."

My patients frequently tell me, "I want to do so many things and do them well, but there's just not enough time!" If I can get them to stop and think about that statement, they see the fallacy quickly. Each twenty-four-hour period contains ample room to maneuver if you have decided what and who are most important and in what order you will distribute your time. My clients are often conflicted because someone gave them the mistaken idea that they can "have it all." But in this culture of overstimulation, no one can possibly have it all. We cannot even have all the *good* things available. "The enemy of the best is often the good," said Theodore Roosevelt, and Thoreau would be astounded at the concept of trying to "have it all." "Simplify, simplify, simplify," he advised.

If the way we allocate our time is a revelation of our values, then the test is whether our schedules mirror our objectives. We can easily allow our calendars to fill with nonessentials until they become cumbersome and unwieldy. Just as a boat needs regular scraping of the barnacles that build up on the hull and impede its speed, so we must haul in our date books regularly to examine them for encrustation. When we do so, we may find an accumulation of obligations there that we never intended, and that slow us in reaching our objectives.

The principle of focus applies very much to balancing our relationships. Some of us spend so many evenings at superficial social affairs that the time we need for friends and extended family gets pinched. We need not accept every social invitation if it has been months since we've sat down for a meal and a good talk with a friend who waters our soul.

I talked once with a nurse who had worked for the same doctor for more than ten years and though he was thirty-five years her senior, she clearly adored him. "I think one reason we have always had such good morale in our office," she said, "is that we all know exactly where we stand with Dr. Whitaker. His priorities are transparent as glass: first comes his wife and children. Those of us on the office staff come next. Our patients are third. And everyone else comes fourth." If there is one single complaint I hear most from women about men, it is, "They're all unwilling to commit." But when a man comes along such as this doctor, with such clear values, he can work hard at a job he likes, and his relationships will thrive as well.

Shifting Gears between Achiever and Nurturer. A young widow sat in my office. She was being rushed by a number of very attractive men but was not impressed. "Here's the problem I have struggled with for years," she said. "In choosing a mate, you can find one who is loving, tender, and caring (a nurturer), or one who is ambitious, achieving, successful (an asserter). But rarely do you find both in the same person. I'm not sure the combination even exists in a man."

We talked around the question for the remainder of the hour, but when the session ended, I let her go knowing I had not been helpful. On the way home that evening I realized what our difficulty had been. Why hadn't I seen it sooner? We had been using the wrong categories! Success at work or love does not depend on the amount of assertiveness or nurturing a person possesses. We are all a mixture of both. The proper category, I realized, was commitment. Advancing in one's career will indeed require a certain amount of assertiveness. And success with friends and family will require shifting gears into a more nurturing, playful mode. But it is not that difficult to make the transition. It simply requires that you be equally committed on each end. At work you focus on one set of goals, and at home you operate with similar focus to accomplish another set of objectives. If you have decided long ago that those two arenas will get your primary attention, you invest your energy accordingly.

Difficulties arise when people make a commitment—consciously or unconsciously—in one place to the neglect of the other. If a man's identity is entirely bound up in his job and he sees his life outside the office as secondary, he will fail to develop the caring skills one needs to sustain a strong marriage or be a good father. And if a woman is working only out of necessity and resents leaving home every day, she will probably fail to develop the skills that could advance her career and eventually make her work more fulfilling.

The Variables and Varieties of a Rich Family Life. Now let's look at some practical ways the person committed to the fast career track can maintain a balanced schedule and develop rich relationships. If you find yourself in a work milieu demanding that you sell your soul for the company, then the solution is simple—though not always easy. You get out. There are plenty of jobs available in enlightened organizations that recognize they will get the best work done if they have emotionally healthy people with strong families, sound friendships, and robust play. But such a drastic step as changing jobs may not be necessary. If you are a productive employee, you probably have more nego-tiating leverage than you realize. Let's say you have a month of business travel and overtime ahead. Perhaps you can negotiate with your superiors about days off later, then explain to your family your plans, the duration of overtime, and how you'll have vacation days accumulated after the rush. Perhaps you will want to propose using those days for a ski trip. Most families can put up with hardship and discomfort as long as they know it is temporary and promises a later reward.

Children like to be out of the house and on the move, and three hours spent at the roller rink may mean more to them than three evenings sitting before the TV at home. Here is another possibility: I know a freelancer who travels a great deal in his work, but who also has considerable flexibility when he is on the road. So when school is not in session or he's working weekends, he often takes one of his children with him. In spare hours the two explore a new city. He says that these interludes of one-on-one contact away from the rest of the family have brought him and each of his children much closer. The possibilities for keeping work and love in balance are more varied than one might expect.

If your family gets too little of your energy, perhaps there are other areas—in addition to work—where you can shave your schedule and reduce your energy drain. In order to afford commodious four-bedroom homes, some young urban couples have located so far out of the city that their commute takes hours and they arrive home exhausted to rebellious children and a strained marriage. Moving to a closer, smaller house could make it possible for the family to have relaxed dinners together and for the parents to help with homework.

It is possible for your schedule to get out of kilter because you're overcommiting yourself to volunteer work, which in itself is entirely worthwhile. If you devote so many hours to church or synagogue meetings that you have little energy left over for your children, you violate God's plan. No matter how many souls you save through your church work, if your family suffers from your absences, you are investing in the wrong place.

When my patients inventory the way they dispense non-working blocks of time, I suggest that they stay on the lookout, not necessarily for the activities that take the most hours but for the ones that sap the most energy. Certain enterprises (perhaps your weekly softball game or quilting group) may relieve tension and actually contribute to your overall well-being. So discard the traditional gauges here. The best contribution you can make to your mate and your children is not necessarily measured by the number of hours you spend with them, but by the amount of energy and interest you give them.

If you have workaholic tendencies, you can enlist your family's aid to curb those habits. Schedules change, and your spouse and children will be flattered if you regularly consult with them as to whether you are using your days disproportionately. Some workaholics stay late at work every evening and go back on weekends not because they ever intended to set such a pattern, or because they particularly like doing so. They developed such a schedule because at some point it was necessary to work overtime; then when the project was finished, leaving at seven instead of five had become habitual. Unfinished work was always there to keep them busy, and their employer began to expect such a schedule. One can gradually become inefficient in time management until evening and weekend hours seem necessary to keep up, and your family or friends can help in reassessing your schedule if you will ask them.

Studies of workaholics seem to indicate that many get satisfaction from their jobs. They love what they do, find their work highly fulfilling, and can get so engrossed at the lab or the plant that they forget to come home for dinner, or maybe for the night. It is the people who must live with workaholics that can become discontented and unhappy. So if you care about both work and your loved ones, log in with the important people on your list, regularly asking whether you are away too much or are too preoccupied with other things when you are with them. In the best marriages, one or the other should ask periodically, "Do you think I'm working too much? Traveling too much? Would you like me to help you more? Are we going out to dinner too much or too little? Would you like to see more movies?

Do we get enough vacations? How can we plan the next year so we have more fun together? Most of all, are we getting enough time to stay tight?"

If your spouse is honest, the answers will vary, because needs and desires vary at different stages and the demands on your mate's schedule shift, just as yours do. You might get a reply such as this: "Right now I have so much to do, that to tell you the truth, when you were gone last week it was a good opportunity to catch up. But this peak period will be over next month, and I'd love to do some extra things with you then."

Balance is never static. Just as runners in a long-distance race must adjust their pace to new terrain, families and friends must stay on the lookout for changes occurring in each other's work loads, and talk frequently about how they can spell each other when someone is under duress at work or school. Love, honor, and negotiate is the key here, as in many things.

The message you want to convey over and over, both with the way you portion out your hours and in what you say is: My work is fulfilling to me (if that is true), but you are everything, and please tell me if you think I seem to put my job ahead of you. In other words, you want to keep declaring, "You are important, and I love you." Even the most surly teenager needs to hear that, whether it appears to register or not.

Step 4. Strengthen your powers of concentration.

The last element in achieving mastery is a concentration that borders on ferocity. When asked, "What do you think is the first requisite for success in your field?" Thomas Edison replied, "The ability to apply your physical and mental energies to one problem incessantly without growing weary." Those at the top usually possess an ability to concentrate that is absent in their lackluster counterparts. This ability can be seen in the way they give themselves whole-heartedly to whatever is before them. Napoleon once boasted that turning from one project to another was like closing a dresser drawer in his mind and opening another.

Not all successful men and women who enjoy their jobs work excessive hours, and if you learn the art of concentration, you could actually reduce your work schedule. According to Henry Ward Beecher, "One intense hour will do more than dreamy years." Certain men and women bring a concentration to their jobs that enables them to accomplish more in four days than others could in seven. A few years ago, our small company hired Douglas Grant, a newly licensed CPA, to help us with our books for the day. I watched this young man as he sat at my partner's desk all morning, poring over the figures without looking up. At noon I said, "Doug, let's get some lunch."

"No, thanks; I'd rather stay here and get this done."

"Well, could we bring you a sandwich?"

"No, thanks."

When we returned, he was still sitting in the same chair, working. And when we went out for a cup of coffee later in the afternoon, he was *still* there. Finally, at about 4:00 p.m. he closed the ledger and said, "Good! Just in time to go to the ball game with my son." At age thirty-nine Grant became chief financial officer of Teledyne, a conglomerate with revenues of more than $3 billion. Is his success due to his brilliance or his ability to focus and get things done? I believe it's more the latter.

And to the fact that he continues to go to ball games with his children. I have followed Grant's career and family life in the ensuing years, and he has continued to balance a commitment to work and family, constantly negotiating his way. For instance, he discovered several years ago that those in his family were not morning people and that he didn't do much "bonding" with them at breakfast, so he leaves for his office at 5:00 a.m. and puts in two productive hours before another person arrives on the executive floor. Then, as a tradeoff, when his children have afternoon games, he leaves at whatever time in the afternoon is necessary. "I know it has irritated some of my bosses when I've missed afternoon meetings," he says, "and who knows? Maybe I've missed a promotion or two, but it's been worth it not to miss those games." The CEO of his company speaks of him with the greatest of admiration—not only for his competence as an executive, but also for his love of family. And I happen to know that he is paid very, very well.

3

THE ART OF SELF-MOTIVATION: EIGHT WAYS TO INCREASE YOUR ENERGY

"Everyone is enthusiastic at times. One person has enthusiasm for 30 minutes, another for 30 days, but it is the person who has it for 30 years who makes a success of life."

—EDWARD B. BUTLER

COMMITMENT RELEASES YOUR INNER ENERGY, AND FOCUS allows you to channel that force in one direction for maximum achievement. In discussing commitment we must now turn to a third topic: overcoming entropy and maintaining our motivation. Certain people seem to wither before our eyes. Others refuse to allow themselves to stagnate and they tap into new sources of inspiration as they go along. Here are some specific things you can do to keep your enthusiasm up and your motivation steady over the long haul:

1. Review and revise your goals constantly.

I once asked Cherry Henricks—who is president of a design firm that started in her home and now occupies seven thousand square feet and employs twenty people—how she keeps up her motivation. "I consider one of my primary tasks to maintain a high level of enthusiasm," she replied. "If I'm motivated, it seems to rub off on the whole staff. And when I'm out of gas, it affects office morale adversely. So I work hard at this, and the best way I know to get refueled is to take some time to set goals—both some large long-range aims and some very specific short-range ones. I write them out in order to be able to refer to them regularly during the week. But even if I never look at the list again, the act of writing these objectives down improves my attitude."

Leaders talk about their goals incessantly. I suspect they do so not only because they want to inspire the people around them, but also because it is an effective technique for self-motivation. Alan Frenier, a columnist for a small Virginia weekly paper, once talked about the value of "going public." He is a recovering alcoholic and, in one of his weekly columns, said so. I asked him if he found this public confession difficult to do. He said he indeed did, but that by making a public pronouncement, he'd discovered a unique method for reinforcing his new-found sobriety. Of course, few of us have newspaper space at our disposal. One can, however, notify several people of important decisions. The principle is the same.

This is one of the places where the integration of work and outside relationships occurs. As we move back and forth, the people we love can be of enormous assistance in our careers. One of the most absurd pieces of advice a counselor could give you is, "Don't talk about work at home. Your family doesn't want to hear your problems at the dinner table." True, you shouldn't turn dinner conversations into gripe sessions—among other things that will convey to your children a negative view of work. But if you have found work you love and if you are enthusiastic about your career, by all means talk about that with your family and other people you care for. By doing this, you are enlisting their aid in clarifying your goals. Also, by asking a friend to be a witness to your objectives, you are employing an age-old technique for motivating yourself. Once you've made some promises to important people, it adds to the reasons to fulfill those dreams. By the same token, you can help breathe new vitality into the motivational systems of your spouse, your children, and your friends by asking them where they want to be five years from now, what their goals are for the second semester, what excites them about their careers.

My friends Charlie and Martha Shedd, who happily raised five children, had the tradition of going around the dinner table each evening to ask, "What was the most exciting thing that happened to you today?" If during such exchanges your children catch some of the fire you have for your job, and hear about some problems they might help you solve, you will have taken a large leap toward building a cohesive family unit. And you will have energized one another.

2. Associate with other energetic, motivated people.

Those with passion like to be around similar persons. They are commited to commitment, so they seek the company of others who take their promises seriously, and when they hire staff, they look not for the most brilliant people but for the most dedicated people.

Could Bill Gates have succeeded in the early days of Microsoft without Paul Allen? Or Allen without Gates? No one knows, but again and again in examining stories of break-through achievement, I found that two or more people were feeding each other's enthusiasm. A remarkable critical mass occurred in which each person performed at a higher level than would have been possible alone.

Winners do not have much patience with uncommitted people, preferring to associate with other passionate individuals—perhaps people who are passionate about totally different projects or causes—because they understand the contagious power of enthusiasm.

This leads to a very practical question: What do we do if we find ourselves living with someone who throws a wet blanket on our enthusiasms and who seems to resent every minute we spend at work if it is not required? Some people regard their mate's boss as their biggest competitor and chip away at any effort their husband or wife expends in trying to advance in business. But smart spouses encourage their mates in their work, for one of the surest ways to have a happy companion in the evenings and on weekends is to have a mate with a successful and fulfilling career.

Criticism about work is also unfortunate because many of us work primarily to provide for the very people who are criticizing us. The first step, then, is to try to determine the reasons your family or friends are negative. When I counsel people in troubled marriages, someone will often say, "I feel torn between trying to do well at my job and being home enough to keep everyone happy there. My family acts as if they hate my company. I don't always like what management puts me through either, but she [or he] never seems to appreciate that I work hard in order to create a good life for our family."

"Have you ever told her that's why you stay so long at the office?" I ask.

"Well, no, but that's obvious, isn't it?"

No, it's not obvious. Our mates cannot read our minds. If we come home exhausted and bedraggled, it is natural for our family to resent a demanding company—especially if we seem cheerful and upbeat when we leave for work each morning. It may appear that indeed we are happiest when we can leave the family difficulties behind and find power and accomplishment in our jobs. So we must declare and re-declare ourselves on this matter: that both career and family are important, but that if ever forced to choose, our loved ones will take precedence every time. Moreover, it is important to explain that one of our biggest motivations for diligent work is this love for our family.

It could be that you are working harder than you wish you had to, when it is not necessary. Often, I find that couples have never sat down and discussed together what standard of living they actually desire. When they talk candidly with each other about this in my office, it frequently turns out that both husband and wife have been working at jobs they hated because they thought their mates wanted a certain cash flow. When in fact the person they love would have preferred to have them home more, living more contentedly on less.

One small way to break down animosity toward your job is to be sure that your family visits your place of work. There was a time—when more people lived on farms and in small towns—that children followed their fathers around the fields, or stopped after school to say hello to them at the bank. But in our modern world, when many of us go off to distant high-rise buildings, children often see those as dark and frightening places that take their moms and dads away from them. (I find that many *couples* have never visited each other's place of business.) A suggestion then: take your children to see what you do and where you do it. Events such as "Take your daughter to work day" can be artificial and boring for your child. But to pick her up for a long lunch and on the way stop by your shop to introduce her to your coworkers and let your daughter see her picture on your desk will make her feel like a princess.

So much for the question of what to do about family systems that drain our energy rather than renew it.

Most people, including those in difficult family situations, have considerable leeway as to where they spend their non-working hours. They know who pulls them down, so to keep their motivation in top form they do not spend large amounts of time with such people. Instead, they go to those who will be inspiriting. This does not mean we should give up all our depressed friends. Dr. Samuel Shoemaker, the great Episcopal clergyman, once said that everyone should take on two or three neurotics—that is, relationships where you never expect to receive as much as you give. "But don't take on too many," he warned, "or they'll suck you down." Negative people need our help, but Shoemaker is right—we must be careful to balance our lives with people who inspire us as well as those we are trying to help.

3. Take time to be with a child.

The next technique for sustaining high energy is closely related to the preceding one. One day St. Francis Xavier retired to his cell exhausted from lack of sleep. He instructed the monks to allow no interruptions. A moment later he came back to clarify his orders: "Of course, if a child comes, please awaken me."

People with balanced lives do not spend many days away from the young. Children energize us in several ways. First, they remind us of nature's fecundity—of the great principle of renewal. At birth, children arrive "trailing clouds of glory," as Wordsworth has it, and simply placing ourselves in contact with this fresh, uninhibited, wide-eyed enthusiasm is restorative. Second, when we hug children and get down on the floor to play with them, it puts us into contact with the childlike tendencies within us and enables us to reach back for the times when we had surging enthusiasms. Jesus was always telling his disciples to be like little children, by which I think he meant, among other things, that the wide-eyed enthusiasm and keen curiosity that children possess are all still available to us.

We were all born idealists and were at first full of hope. But then as we grew a little older, something happened— we began to learn about disappointment. Perhaps we were exuberant at the prospect of going to the beach, then the trip was canceled. Or our parents were divorced and we peered out the window on a Saturday, waiting for a father who never came as promised. We began the semester with a resolution to get all A's and somehow the plan went awry. Such frustrations can cause us to fear wanting too much and feel foolish about having too much enthusiasm. The disappointments have hurt too keenly and we scale down our hopes.

But the fire never goes completely out, and to spend hours with a young child who still has a love of life and zest for the future can help fan our own embers back into a flame.

4. Refuse to see yourself as victim.

When one examines those who understand the mechanics of self-motivation, another characteristic stands out: these people believe that for the most part they have the power to control their destinies. If you are a fatalist, it will be difficult to keep yourself inspired to go the second mile, because fatalists can summon little hope for the future.

The high achievers' commitment seems rooted in their basic belief system about how the universe works. These hard-headed believers have acquired—sometimes by a fluke—the conviction that they are in the driver's seat and that they have control over their circumstances.

Richard Logan found in his study of individuals who survived severe physical ordeals—polar explorers wandering alone in the Arctic, concentration camp inmates—that they shared an implicit belief in their power to take destiny in their own hands. They did not doubt that their own resources gave them the freedom to determine their fates.

We therapists hear many stories of how people have been victimized, how they've had a succession of bad breaks and are the product of "dysfunctional" homes. On my good days I'm sympathetic and try to hear them out, to encourage catharsis for their pain, then gradually lead them into a problem-solving mode. But some days I mutter to myself that if another patient comes in the door and says one word about being the product of a dysfunctional family, I'm going to stand up and do something dysfunctional to them. *All* families are dysfunctional at times. And biography is filled with the stories of people who overcame the most miserable of environments.

Here is a remarkable case of a girl from a very dysfunctional home. Her name is Maya. An African-American girl whose parents are divorced, she spends most of her childhood living with her grandmother in a tightly segregated Arkansas town. The child is tall, thin as a stick, always breaking things. She has a rebellious streak. When she is eight, her mother's boyfriend rapes her and she spends days near death in a St. Louis hospital. Then, when she recovers, she is virtually mute for more than a year.

Later, the girl is shipped to San Diego to spend the summer with her father; she gets into a fight with his girlfriend and is badly cut. This time, no one takes her to a hospital. She flees out the back door and sleeps in a junkyard car for a full month. ("It wasn't so bad," she said later. "Several runaway kids were living in the junkyard, and as long as we made ourselves scarce during the daytime, the employees looked the other way.")

By age nineteen, she is a single mother with a three-year-old son, and is experimenting with drugs. She has fallen in love with a pimp, and to please him she is trying to learn to become a prostitute.

Anyone in my profession, looking at a psychological history such as this would think there was small hope for this girl, and would predict a precipitous decline during what would probably be a very short life. But it happens that inside this young woman lay forces stronger than any of the manacles of the underclass. Among other things, there was her zealous love of poetry, and eventually, through a circuitous path filled with setbacks, she became a poet instead of a prostitute.

Now fast forward forty years. The place is Washington, D.C. The date is January 20, 1993. The occasion is the inaugural ceremony for a new president of the United States. The woman who has been commissioned to read an inaugural poem is Maya Angelou. It is *Doctor* Maya Angelou now. She is the Reynolds Professor at Wake Forest University, author of nine books, and the recipient of numerous awards. When this regal woman, now in her sixties, stepped to the podium and began to read in her deep, melodious voice, "On the Pulse of Morning," it evoked strong emotion in millions of us sitting before our TV screens. And it exposed the lie of Freudian fatalism that says you must be the prisoner of your early circumstances.

It would be foolhardy to minimize the economic and cultural forces that cripple our urban poor, or to argue that no circumstances lie beyond our control. But in light of the accomplishments of people such as Dr. Angelou, it would also be foolhardy to deny individual responsibility. No matter how miserable a hand we have been dealt, we have within us the power to create our destinies, to determine our futures.

5. Learn to think of yourself as a problem solver.

"Efficiency in industry," says Sir John H. Jones, who is chairman of Imperial Chemical Industries, one of England's largest conglomerates, "is looking at a mess, diagnosing a way out, writing an instant book on the problem, and the moment you are finished, tearing it up because the next problem's going to be different."

Jones began working for the company at a salary of £800 a year, and his first assignment was, quite literally, garbage. Wilton, a huge Imperial Chemical complex covering thirty-five hundred acres, had an incinerator that was supposed to burn all its waste material but was not coping. "They were planning to build a new one so they didn't want to spend any money on it," Jones later explained. "I went down early one morning, and I could not see the incinerator. It was hidden under mountains of rubbish. By lunch time it was quite obvious to me that the real problem was that the chaps were not putting the right stuff in. They were lazing around; there was just no method. The mixtures of waste were wrong, some burnt well, some badly. Put too much in and the thing went out." So Jones buckled down and worked flat out for three days, sixteen or seventeen hours a day. When he went back to his boss, he handed in his report and said, "Oh, by the way, we have run out of material to burn."

Jones' first assignment was, quite literally, garbage.

Soon Jones gained a reputation as a troubleshooter and rose very rapidly in his company, eventually becoming its head. When asked about his success, Jones always depreciates his intelligence. But he is quite frank in saying that he has an unusual ability to solve problems.

Some time ago I discovered a statement by Robert Updegraff, an early management consultant. I have used this quotation at hundreds of management seminars and motivational talks to sales representatives. I have quoted it in speeches all over the world. Here is the gauntlet Updegraff threw down:

> You ought to be glad for the troubles on your job because they provide about half your income. If it were not for the things that go wrong, the difficult

people with whom you deal, and the problems of your working day, someone could be found to handle your job for half of what you are being paid. So start looking for more troubles. Learn to handle them cheerfully and with good judgment, as opportunities rather than irritations, and you will find yourself getting ahead at a surprising rate. For there are plenty of big jobs waiting for people who are not afraid of troubles.

When we throw ourselves into a difficulty that others have found unsolvable it multiplies our powers, brings out the best in us, and refuels our motivation. Those who shirk challenges in order to conserve their energies need to know that energy cannot be hoarded. For human beings are not the kind of machines that wear out from overuse. They wear out from lack of use.

6. Maintain a course midway between boredom and stress.

For more than twenty years psychologist Mihaly Csikszentmihalyi has been studying people who have peak experiences—what he has come to call "flow." He asks people to tell how it felt when their lives were at their fullest, when what they did was most enjoyable. The respondents included surgeons, professors, young mothers, teenagers, and the sample drew from Korea, Japan, Thailand, and a Navajo reservation, as well as from traditional American and European cultures.

The reports were remarkably similar. A dancer immersed in an intricate performance, a long-distance swimmer crossing the English Channel, and a chess player during a tournament told the same story: they had periods when time seemed to stand still and they were devoid of self-consciousness. Athletes occasionally talk about the "zone," where they are so perfectly tuned to their game that the ball seems to slow down and they can actually see the seams as it comes to them.

Dr. Csikszentmihalyi found that we are most likely to operate at such peak levels when we confront tasks that use all our abilities, but which we have at least a good chance of completing. Ecstasy can come for no apparent reason—a bar of haunting music may trigger it, or a wonderful view—but by far the most optimal experiences are reported within sequences of activities that are goal-directed and bounded by rules. "Enjoyment," says Csikszentmihalyi, "appears at the boundary between boredom and anxiety, when the challenge is just balanced with the person's capacity to act." If the tennis game is close, and we have a chance of winning yet cannot win easily, then we can play with passion. The ideal, then, is to raise our expectations gradually as our skills increase, so we're neither pushed to the limit nor coasting.

This is quite different from an old canard, found in many success manuals, that said, "If someone asks if you can do a job, tell them 'Yes,' then when you get the assignment find out how to do it." In our technologically intricate world, such a careless policy can get you into trouble. The ideal is a healthy gap between aspiration and achievement. "It's a tricky balancing act," says social psychologist Gilbert Brim, "and it's one we engage in almost daily as we keep testing ourselves and readjusting our level of 'just manageable difficulty.'"

7. Reach for the energy available on the second mile.

It is a truism that those who excel are always eager to go the second mile. Jesus has done us a favor to distinguish, in the Sermon on the Mount, between one-mile people and second-mile people. In the first category are those who work with one eye on the clock and give their job exactly what is expected—no more and no less. Such persons are to be pitied, for their work will be a drudgery and the clock will crawl. In the second category are those who seem eager to reach for more responsibilities and new problems to solve—to give more than is asked.

We admire this second category of people, and as everyone knows, they are the ones who, when promotions are handed out, will most likely advance. But they do not go this extra distance merely because they seek advancement. They do it because they know energy and enjoyment are to be found during the second mile. It is on the stretch after the first milepost that extra motivation and personal power become available.

At first this seems a paradox. When the average person is exhausted at the end of a mile, how is it that other people can find a second wind by doubling the distance? In my survey I found that highly successful people were, without exception, more energetic than normal, but they seemed to create this energy by sheer will power and by employing certain techniques such as thinking of themselves as problem solvers and deliberately going the second mile.

The reason for finding energy during the second mile lies in the sense of freedom that comes when we pass the point we are forced to go, then choose to go further. With this choice, our commitment suddenly increases. Here it is worthwhile to look again at Csikszentmihalyi's research. He found that one of the ingredients for "flow" was a belief that you are in control—or at least the belief that you could *gain* control over a set of circumstances. The first mile— forced on us by some authority figure—is hard. But when we make the choice to go a second, we are now in charge and we find our energy heightened.

This principle is best illustrated by a story one of my old professors was fond of telling. As a small boy he was asked by his mother, on a hot day, to go out and pick a pail full of blackberries. "I trudged out reluctantly," he says, "and had my pail only half full when I was already tired and wanting to go back into the cool house. Then the thought occurred to me, 'I'll pick two pails and surprise my mother.' Suddenly," he said, "there was lift to my step, and an energy in my work. I'll never forget my mother's delighted look that afternoon and the family's praise at dinner. But I've too frequently forgotten the lesson I learned that day: that it is when going the second mile that you move from what is required to what is enjoyed, and it is during the second mile that you discover a surge of strength."

Harry Emerson Fosdick writes wisely on how this principle applies in families:

There are few things more pathetic than a one-mile family where members of the family only do for each other what is required. Parents put food on the table, the children are provided for, abuse is avoided. But anyone who has had a real mother or father knows that such a description leaves the glory out. The real parents do their duties too, but there is something more—a radiance that glows through the simple tasks like a quiet dawn in summer, an ampleness of love. Some say of their duties, "I must," some say "I ought," but Heaven be thanked for those mothers and fathers, those husbands and wives who say, "I love you, so I want to give." One is the slave of necessity, the other the grim moralist doing one's duty, the other a person of abounding sense of privilege in life, who feels the pleasure of living not for how much you can hoard but how much you can give.

A young woman who had worked her way up in a small high-tech company and hit the infamous "glass ceiling," says that she went about changing jobs like this: "I chose two companies in Boston, either of which I'd have given my eye teeth to work for, and when I got to the vice presidents, I made basically the same pitch. I said, 'When I sat in your chair hiring people—though in a much smaller company—I always had some humungous problem that I wished some-body would walk in the door and have the ability to take off my hands. Do you have any such situations? If so, I'd like to ask for the job.' In both cases the vice presidents thought awhile and answered almost the same: 'As a matter of fact, I do.' And both of them made me an offer within the week."

Why was she so quickly hired? Doubtless because those executives wanted an employee unafraid to take on tough problems. But probably because they also realized that here was a person who knew the art of self-motivation and who liked to work in the space where the second wind comes.

8. Replenish your spiritual reserves.

When we examine carefully the sources of strength in the great achievers through history, we discover that a startling number had some set of religious beliefs and practices strong as an oak. Perhaps they had reservations about orga-nized religion, and perhaps they did not talk a lot about their faith, but they were fed by a subterranean stream of spiritual power that ran deep and made no noise. If you have a belief system, then by all means take advantage of it for self-motivation. Because if we look exclusively to our-selves for inspiration, we will often find the cupboard bare; on the other hand, if we plant ourselves next to the streams of renewing water that are available from God, fresh nutri-ents are always available.

This will require far more than going to a house of worship, valuable as that is. We must not confuse spirituality with attendance at church, serving on committees, or teaching classes. When we do so, our church activities may actually get in the way of spiritual power. As Jesus made clear, most of our prayer should be in private, and if he himself required so much time alone with God to recharge his batteries, we certainly do as well.

Those who in Emerson's noble phrase, "live from a great depth of being," have always been people of prayer. The *New York Times* says that the revival of interest in prayer is "the most powerful, least documented development within American religion today." Rather than the outward manifestations that marked earlier movements, the newer phase "emphasizes the interior nurture of the soul and deepening of faith," according to the newspaper.

A cautionary word is in order here. If devotional practices are merely a "technique" for pumping ourselves up and making more sales that day, it will backfire. The paradox is that if we worship God because God is God—and for no other pragmatic reason—then the byproducts are enormous.

Several thousand years ago, a poet mused over the topic before us: the remarkable difference in people's growth patterns. Why do some wither "like chaff that the wind drives away"? And why do others thrive, continuing to grow year after year? It is because the latter are linked to God, says Psalm 1:

> They are like trees
> planted by streams of water,
> which yield their fruit in its season,
> and their leaves do not wither.
> In all that they do, they prosper.

PART TWO
DISCIPLINE

4

THE RICH
REWARDS OF
SELF-DISCIPLINE

"Without self-discipline, there is no life at all."

—KATHERINE HEPBURN

SELF-DISCIPLINE. THE VERY TERM CONJURES UP NEGATIVE images to some—pictures of colorless drones whose only facial expression is a pinched seriousness. Moreover, the term can conjure up guilt feelings. "I'm tired of people telling me I have potential and could do so much if I were just more disciplined," a patient will say. "Everybody would like to have more willpower, but I haven't found a way to learn it, and pep talks like that just get me depressed."

In this and the following chapter, I will offer some practical ideas about how to cultivate the virtue of self-discipline, for it, like most habits, can be learned. The topic is important because if you develop discipline it will help you succeed better in the two areas under consideration: work and love. Moreover, it will assist you in keeping those two areas in a balanced symmetry.

Let's consider work first. Irwin C. Hansen, chief executive officer of Summit Medical Center in Oakland, California, has gained a national reputation for turning around under-performing hospitals. But Hansen has not always seen himself as a winner. In fact, like Albert Einstein, he had a slow start. When forced to repeat the third grade, it was humiliating, and only years later did he discover that he was dyslexic. Though most who know Hansen today call him "a brilliant problem-solver," he still doesn't consider himself unusually talented. "You don't need talent to succeed," he growls. "All you need is a big pot of glue. You smear some on your chair and some on the seat of your pants, and you sit down."

He wasn't exaggerating. Many people achieve extraordinary things simply because they stay glued to their chairs; they tough it out through the difficult periods when inspiration is lacking and everyone else has quit for the day. And what gives them the stamina to do that? A belief in deferred gratification. They know that to move toward distant goals it is often necessary to postpone pleasure. This belief that you reap what you sow is what sustains the violinist practicing alone year after year, the athlete enduring long workouts in the weight room, the manager consistently getting projects done on time and on budget.

Two current trends make self-discipline a more valuable commodity than ever before. The first is that we are gaining more and more flexibility for employment. Almost 8 million people now telecommute and another 40 million hold full- or part-time home-based jobs. With such freedom, these workers report, it is easy to wander into the kitchen for a cup of coffee and end up watching two hours of TV. Whether we excel will depend in considerable part on our ability to summon the self-discipline to stay in the chair.

The second trend is that baby boomers will make up about 50% of the work force in the early years of the twenty-first century and will be at stages in their careers where they have the greatest expectations of moving up. But given the combination of this population bulge and the simultaneous downsizing of businesses, the boomers' rise will be slow, and the generation behind them will be backing up with increasing pressure. Career grid locks will occur frequently, many moves will be lateral, and most people will be forced to spend a great deal of time on a plateau. Those who continue honing their skills while on this plateau will be the ones who eventually get to the top.

Patient on the Plateaus

The plateau and its conquest deserves examination. George Leonard, in his superb book *Mastery: The Keys to Success and Long-Term Fulfillment* (New York: Dutton, 1991), uses martial arts and other sports as an example of what it takes to excel, but the laws for success he examines in athletics will work in almost all fields. Progress, he says, will consist of ". . . relatively brief spurts of progress, each of which is followed by a slight decline to a plateau. . . ."

Figure 1. The Master

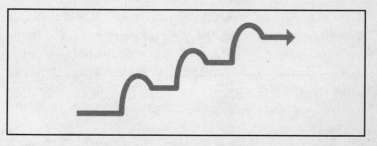

But most people never achieve mastery. Instead, they fall into several other categories:

Figure 2. The Dabbler

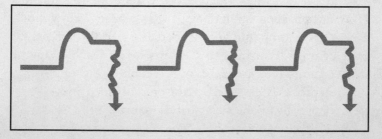

When we consider Leonard's diagram of the Dabbler's progress, we recognize instantly its accuracy. We have all known people who took up some new hobby, for instance, with high enthusiasm. They bought all the equipment, subscribed to all the magazines on the subject, and could talk of nothing else. But then when they hit the plateau and their progress flattened, they began to lose interest, started to skip practices, and eventually decided it wasn't the right avocation for them after all.

The same thing applies to careers, according to Leonard. "The Dabbler loves new jobs, new offices, new colleagues. He sees opportunities at every turn. He salivates over projected earnings." But then the plateau occurs. The Dabblers cannot endure the tough periods when there are no accolades and no promotions.

We meet the Dabblers in relationships as well. They are likely to flee when a relationship gets rocky. It is impossible for two people to live in the same house or work at adjoining cubicles for any extended time without negative electricity occasionally occurring. Working out the conflicts, enduring the dry spells when you give more than you receive, learning to forgive—all are hard work, and the Dabbler often does not have the staying power required.

"The Dabbler," says Leonard, "specializes in honeymoons. He revels in seduction and surrender, the telling of life stories, the display of love's tricks and trappings. . . . When the initial ardor begins to cool, he starts looking around." It takes too much effort to keep the relationship growing, and the Dabbler begins to lose heart. "How much easier it is to jump into another bed and start the process all over again," according to Leonard. "The Dabbler might think of himself as an adventurer, a connoisseur of novelty, but he's probably closer . . . to the eternal kid. Though partners change, he or she stays just the same."

Next, we have the Obsessive:

Figure 3. The Obsessive

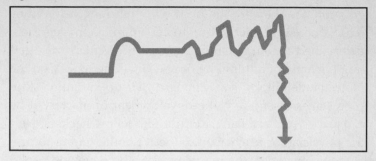

Obsessives are another story altogether. Upon hitting the inevitable plateau, they do not give up and start a new undertaking. Instead, they become fanatical about progressing. "He stays after class talking to the instructor. He asks what books and tapes he can buy to help him make progress faster," says Leonard. "But when he inevitably regresses and finds himself on a plateau, he simply won't accept it. He redoubles his effort. He pushes himself mercilessly. He refuses to accept his boss's and colleagues' counsel of moderation. He works all night at the office. . . ."

"Somehow, in whatever he is doing, the Obsessive manages for a while to keep making brief spurts of upward progress, followed by sharp declines—a jagged ride toward a sure fall. When the fall occurs, the Obsessive is likely to get hurt. And so are friends, colleagues, stockholders, and lovers."

But the worst group of all may be the Hackers:

Figure 4. The Hacker

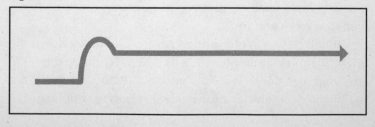

Hackers, or what we might call Coasters, have a different attitude. They are the ones who quit long before they retire. There is no motivating force within that makes them determined to continue moving upward. "After sort of getting the hang of a thing, he or she is willing to stay on the plateau indefinitely," says Leonard. "He doesn't mind skipping stages essential to the development of mastery if he can just go out and hack around with fellow hackers. He's the physician or teacher who doesn't bother going to professional meetings, the tennis player who develops a solid forehand and figures he can make do with a ragged backhand. At work, he does only enough to get by, leaves on time or early, takes every break, talks instead of doing his job, and wonders why he doesn't get promoted."

"There's really no way around it," says Leonard. "To take the master's journey, you have to practice diligently, striving to hone your skills, to attain new levels of competence. But while doing so—and this is the inexorable fact of the journey—you also have to be willing to spend most of your time on a plateau, to keep practicing even when you seem to be getting nowhere."

The Beliefs Behind Self-Discipline

The law of deferred gratification, as solid as the laws of astronomy, is fundamental to the development not only of self-discipline but also to many of the other habits we are discussing. We will find this principle at work in all the best relationships, enabling people to maintain a life centered between work and love.

It will be worth our while, therefore, to break down the principle and look at some of its individual components. "We are what we believe," Chekov once wrote, and those who are willing to defer gratification believe at least four things:

Belief #1: Most success builds slowly.

Balanced people are suspicious of get-rich-quick schemes, instant solutions to complex problems, overnight intimacy, and all the flash and clutter that accrues from the worship of quick success. These men and women know they are more likely to get ahead gradually, steadily building one accomplishment upon another. They don't expect the world to fall into their laps. It never has. So they don't worry if they are not rising as quickly as the *wunderkinder*. They understand cumulative power: constructing a great building one brick at a time, winning football games one play at a time, building a clientele one call at a time.

If you are a disciplined person, you take seriously the law of cumulative power. You know that great achievements are the sum of details. Lots of people take the first step. But the peak performers are those who move forward slowly and tenaciously, knowing that with each additional step they are enhancing the value of the first.

Les Krull, superintendent of a large Hallmark Card plant in Topeka, Kansas, told me that when he interviews job applicants he looks at their track records to see if they follow this principle of postponed rewards. "For instance," he said, "it's not essential that our employees have a college degree. But the character traits that the degree reveals are essential. I want someone who, when others were dropping out of school to make money and drive new cars, resisted the temptation to quit. They stayed in school, drove old cars if necessary, and endured temporary hardships because they knew it would bring dividends later. We want people with that philosophy—people who take the long view."

This basic belief in the rewards of tenacity applies equally to friendships. Good friendships are not constructed in a day, a week, or even in a year. We are suspicious of anyone who tells us his or her whole life story during the first hour after our meeting. Trust accrues gradually as we try pieces of intimate information on friends and watch how they handle them. Whether they are shocked, or whether they lecture us. Whether they keep confidences. Whether they seem to continue enjoying our company when they know the worst about us. And whether they take the risk of telling us similar kinds of potentially damaging information. If trust builds slowly, we must give high priority to the time it requires. We're talking here about more than the time to go to an occasional ball game with your friend. We're talking about long walks together when you talk at length, evenings when the TV is off and you let down your reserves far into the night. You must have love to live, and you don't build love with marathon days at the office during the week and casual socializing on the weekends.

Nourishing friendships are sustained not only by talk; they are also sustained by acts of kindness and by gifts of one's time—helping your friend move, spending a Saturday reshingling the neighbor's roof, going to a birthday party for an acquaintance where you won't know anyone else. Or you take a lunch hour to purchase books for two people you care about, and you have the books gift wrapped and sent to your friends' offices. These are acts that will linger in memory for years. They put love in the bank and help sustain the relationship when expenditures exceed income.

No one is saying that the construction of a balanced existence is easy, but one thing is clear: until we learn self-discipline, we will never be able to remain centered for long. Keeping your life in proportion requires patience and it requires regular negotiation and renegotiation among at least three forces: the inner set of priorities and values you have set for yourself, the demands of your career, and the fluctuating needs of the people you love. In juggling these forces, the balanced individual forsakes immediate gratification and looks at the bigger picture. If, for instance, you know you'd win immediate points with your boss (and perhaps even a bonus) by working seven days a week for six weeks, you would sign up if short-term goals were your only criteria. But if your friends or family are going to need large chunks of your time during that six weeks, the decision is not difficult. Jobs come and go. Friends and family are for a lifetime.

Belief #2: Feelings are an imperfect guide to conduct.

At first blush, this belief—and for that matter the emphasis of this entire chapter—may seem almost diametrically opposed to the passion and enthusiasm I advocated in the previous three chapters. To have urged upon us both enthusiasm and self-discipline may appear to be confusing and contradictory. But I hope to show, before we are finished, that self-discipline will make you a free person rather than a dull drone. Moreover, a fire in the belly to achieve something great should not be confused with the hedonistic slavery to feelings that causes some people to pinball back and forth with every tilt of mood, and that creates so much havoc in our world.

In battling our current drug subculture, the problem is not primarily poverty or inadequate police enforcement. It is the widespread belief in immediate gratification and a worship of feelings: if something makes you feel better, it must be good.

New York clergyman Harry Emerson Fosdick once related an incident from his boyhood that drove home the truth that feelings are an imperfect guide to behavior. Fosdick's father, a high school principal, said to his wife as he left for work one morning, "Tell Harry that he can cut the grass today if he feels like it." Then, after walking a few steps down the street he called back, "And tell Harry he had better feel like it." Fosdick says that the sound of that instruction never quite left him. "For instance," he says, "facing another sermon's preparation I have heard my father's voice, 'Tell Harry he can cut the grass if he feels like it. And he'd better feel like it.'"

There is routine grass-cutting in every vocation. No matter how thrilling the high spots, one's calling is like an iceberg—the peak is visible but most of it is a bulk of details under water, invisible, routine, uninspiring. Our ability to function well in those unseen areas, to carry out the unheralded routine work whether we feel like it or not, can determine our destiny.

Among the forces that work against self-discipline and balance is the longing for pleasure. Some moralists try to minimize the ecstasy, color, and allure of what Freud called the Pleasure Principle. But the Bible does not say that sin is unattractive, or that pleasure is easy to resist; it only says that the pleasures of sin are temporary and the rewards of self-discipline are permanent. The natural inclination to seek fun is not in itself bad, but if allowed to control our lives, it leads to dangerous consequences.

Anyone who has crafted a long friendship or a solid family knows the distinction between fun and happiness. Love is too often regarded as some flow of feelings to which we abandon ourselves, having no connection to rationality. When in fact love requires at times that we sacrifice, that we refuse to allow ourselves to be governed by our feelings and the desire for pleasure. Raising children can scarcely be called "fun" at every juncture. There are periods when it is demanding, draining, grueling, grubby work. But when you are hugging your daughter and tucking her into bed, or watching her graduate from school, your happiness far outweighs the temporary pleasure you passed up.

If a marriage has grown routine and boring, an affair might seem to be more exciting. But self-disciplined persons pass up such excitement because they know what carnage it can wreak on their partners or on their children. They forgo the lure of the immediate to build a family in which love is constant.

I know an outgoing man who likes people in general and women in particular. He has a wife whom he loves, but he says that every few years he meets a new woman, or finds himself suddenly involved with a woman he has known for a time—and falls in love. The chemistry, he tells me, is often strong, and the only thing he can do is pull back. Sometimes the woman does not know why he has suddenly turned cool. "It always hurts," he says, "and I dally with the fantasy that I could have this romantic fling without jeopardizing what my wife and I have together—so long as she didn't find out. But afterwards, when the intensity of the desire subsides, I'm always glad I didn't do it." Millions of husbands and wives who happily sit around their kitchen tables with the families they love can reflect on how close they came to jeopardizing it all, grateful that they stayed on the disciplined path rather than allowing their feelings to guide their conduct.

Belief #3: The human organism is at its best not when we indulge it but when we stretch it.

We were created to be remarkably elastic. When you reflect on the increased capability in, say, a weight lifter who at first cannot press 125 pounds and after a year's training can press 250 pounds, it becomes clear that you have considerable capacity for stretching. When you are a runner and break some record, you know you did it because in the previous months you were still running wind sprints when everyone else had gone home. Or when you win a prize in English, you know you won because you kept revising your essay when you were sick of the thing, fed up with the material, and screaming to be rid of it. Let's say you are a pianist, bored with exercises. Then an inspiring teacher persuades you to stay on the bench for a few more hours. When you break through the boredom, you discover you are capable of far more than you believed, and you reap the results of that discipline by playing a beautiful sonata you thought was beyond your ability.

These are the habits that eventually separate the amateurs from the masters. The amateur lacks the self-discipline to continue working away to pull out from the pack and achieve a lead—that slight lead that makes you better than a thousand other oboe players, that gives your trumpet tone that slight improvement over the crowds of amateur trumpet players, that enables you to complete a surgical procedure three minutes faster than anyone else. Consistently, every time. A part of such achievement is talent. But a larger part is the belief that you are at your best when you are stretching.

When Mike Schmidt retired from baseball in 1987, he had been the National League's Most Valuable Player three times, one of the preeminent home-run hitters in baseball history, and a great fielder. The winter before his last season, he could usually be found at 7:45 a.m. on cold, steel gray days at Pat Croce's workout center near his home, going through one of the most grueling workouts ever designed. Sportswriter Glen Waggoner, watching him there, commented: "It will be Schmidt's last season. He will hit his five-hundredth career home run in the spring no matter how many leg lifts he does this winter. The man will make $2 million during the summer, just for putting on his jockstrap 162 times. He doesn't need to be in *good* shape, much less *great* shape to play baseball. So why bother?"

Schmidt said, "Look, I know that I'm part of two or three percent of 600 major-league players who are working out right now, trying to get themselves into the best possible physical and mental condition to play baseball to the best of their abilities. Most guys just lollygag through baseball, getting by on their talent, which they had nothing to do with."

The athlete had lots of ups and lots of downs in his career: "I know what it's like to strike out four times on twelve pitches, and what it's like to hit four home runs in a game," he said. "I know how it feels to go one for twenty in a World Series, and to be World Series MVP. I know what it's like to be booed by fifty thousand people, and what it's like to be cheered by them."

A certain elegant poise marks Schmidt's style of life. To what does he attribute his staying power? Two things turned him around: he met and married Donna Wightman, and, in his words, "I came to grips with my Christian commitment." It is an enlightening statement. A combination of a rich family love, and a strong set of religious values. It is about as good a list as we can compile for the primary ingredients of success, the bedrock that enables a person to stay on the monotonous plateaus and continue stretching, even when they boo you, even when your game has deteriorated.

Belief #4: Discipline leads to freedom.

Konrad Adenauer, who between 1949 and 1963 was Chancellor of West Germany and one of the architects of the amazing rebirth of his nation, in an article entitled "The Best Advice I Ever Had," tells of the influence of his father, who imbued in him the motto, "To the last mile—and enjoy it."

Like most youngsters, Adenauer would have preferred playing ball to conjugating Latin verbs, but his father insisted that mastering his studies must come first. "'Concentrate,' he urged me, his pointed beard bristling with earnestness. 'Do not let yourself be diverted until you are finished—not even if a cannon goes off at your elbow.'" Despite his father's earnestness about work, Adenauer says their home was not a gray, joyless place—it rang with laughter and the sounds of well earned good times.

When Adenauer arrived at the University of Munich, his clear duty was to complete his studies as soon as possible in order to help support the family. "Night after night I studied a law book by the light of a petroleum lamp," he writes. "When I felt I absolutely had to go to sleep, I would remember my father's advice and carry on, but how could I 'go the last mile' every night?

"When my heavy head drooped with sleepiness, I plunged my feet into the cold water and shocked myself awake."

Then it came to me. I filled my porcelain wash-basin with water and put it on the floor beside me, took off my shoes and read on, barefoot. When my heavy head drooped with sleepiness, I plunged my feet into the cold water and shocked myself awake. Thanks to this stratagem, I finished the University in three years instead of four."

Adenauer reports that his father's counsel not only helped him in the University, but in many ways throughout his career: "I have never kept office hours. I have found that if you want to go the last mile, you don't hear the clock strike six any more than you hear the cannon at your elbow. Most of the happiness in what to me has been a very happy life, has come, I believe, from the times I have 'gone the last mile,' and done a job fully."

What should not be missed here is Adenauer's conclusion that self-discipline can lead to freedom and happiness. Let's say you are the musician we referred to earlier, going over and over the same exercise, enduring the boredom of hours of practice. What eventually happens is that your fingers acquire the muscle memory to do the exercise perfectly. That skill is a necessary prerequisite for learning more intricate exercises, and enables you to break through to the next level. You are compounding your abilities and opening up a whole new world of freedom.

The president of a multi-level marketing business said, "I get very upset at the get-rich-quick books that never talk about the long hours and the hard work usually required for success. I also feel sad at the number of people in our business who say, 'It doesn't matter how hard I work, I'm not ever going to become a success.' Those individuals give up before they've allowed their investment to bear fruit," he observes. "What they don't realize in the early years of their business is that, even though they may not be making a lot of money, they're developing their talents and accumulating knowledge, getting a little better at what they do with every year."

"True," the executive said, "all that knowledge and development may not pay off today or tomorrow, but the more you do, the more you keep building your talents, wisdom, and freedom. Eventually the payoff will be more than you ever anticipated—both in terms of money and in terms of incredible business success."

5

SIX STRATEGIES FOR IMPROVING YOUR SELF-DISCIPLINE

After a performance someone said to the pianist Paderewski, "Mr. Paderewski, you are a genius." He replied, "Madam, that may be true now. But before I was a genius, I was a drudge."

WE HAVE BEEN DISCUSSING THE PRINCIPLE OF POSTPONED pleasure and the assumptions on which it is based. Now we turn to some practical suggestions for making yourself a more disciplined person and thereby balancing your life.

1. Set positive goals with attainable subsets and intermediate rewards.

As I help my patients work on self-discipline, I find that it is easy for them to fall into several pitfalls.

For one thing, their plans for self-improvement are often so negative that they are doomed to fail. They promise themselves, "I will stop working so many hours, I will stop smoking and criticizing my children, I will lose weight, I will cut down on my drinking and quit procrastinating." No one can become very disciplined when he or she has such a negative plan. The secret is to strengthen your good habits and add positive ones, gradually weakening and eliminating the bad ones by displacement.

The second mistake my patients make is that their aspirations are too general. There is a vast difference between having fantasies and having a plan. We all know people who have pie-in-the-sky dreams. They wish they had lots of money, they wish they had more time for their friends, they wish they were famous, they wish they could afford a vacation home. This is hot tub talk.

Goals are quite different. They are specific. One entrepreneur I interviewed says, "Having a goal helps you measure your progress. In other words, it keeps you from cheating. It's one thing to say, 'Today I'm going to improve.' There is no real way to measure that at the end of the day. But if your goal is to talk to four prospective new clients today, you have a clear way to keep score."

That man's remark illustrates the third pitfall you can fall into: your objectives can be so grand that when you see little progress you quickly become discouraged. People say to me, "I have made a thousand sets of resolutions and it's always a joke. I don't know how many times I've bought a membership in a gym, gone every day for a week, then never gone back. What's wrong with me?" There's nothing wrong with them. They simply have not appreciated how resistant the human organism is to change, and they have set goals far too large. To go from no exercise to a strenuous program of daily workouts is a revolutionary move. You are not only taxing your body, but also asking for a large outlay of time and a radical change in your daily routine. Ordinarily we can't change that quickly. So instead of aiming for quick self-reformation, aim for gradual progress. Much better to begin by walking a half mile every other day. When you've stayed with that plan for a few weeks, you may be ready to increase the distance and frequency. But in the meantime, you can congratulate yourself that you laid down a mark with a reasonable, reachable objective, and did what you set out to do. As in most things, success breeds success.

Building In Intermediate Rewards

A woman who now owns her own computer repair company says her first year in college was miserable: "I had never been on my own before. There was nobody to tell me to get my homework done, nobody to tell me whether to go to class or stay home when I had a cold. The result was that my life was a shambles. I tried to study in the apartment, and it never worked. I'd read for half an hour, hear something on TV that sounded interesting, and end up watching dumb stuff all afternoon. Then I'd have to stay up until 2:00 a.m. to get ready for a test. Work and relaxation bled together, and whenever I goofed off, I felt guilty because I wasn't studying.

"That summer I took a seminar on 'How to Succeed in College,' and it was all about time management. So in the fall, when I went back to school, I set a goal of studying six hours every day at the library, and when those six hours were logged in—even if I hadn't mastered all the material—I went home and rewarded myself by watching TV or going out for a pizza. What a difference! Now I didn't feel guilty. I had worked hard for six hours, though it had been painful to stick it out and hard to resist the temptation to indulge myself. Now, in all good conscience, I could put my feet up and really enjoy watching a video. Best of all, my grades improved tremendously. I'm convinced that I own my own company and have sixteen people working for me now, not because I'm smarter than most people, but because I learned self-discipline in college."

> "Now, in all good conscience, I could put my feet up and really enjoy watching a video."

Perhaps the most significant thing about this woman's system for self-improvement is that she rewarded herself for the self-discipline on the spot. It is a tenet of behavior modification that positive behavior needs immediate reward. In her case the college diploma was too far off. So was the grade at the end of the quarter. What she did was to reward herself for the *study* each day, and eventually the grades and the diploma took care of themselves.

A last comment on goal-setting: Do not berate yourself for all your abandoned resolutions. Rather than kicking yourself for the shortfall, congratulate yourself that you are still striving. This especially applies to the issue of keeping love and work in balance. No matter how resolutely we have determined to stay centered, to be more attentive to our mates, more forgiving toward our children, more patient with our aged parents, we will in a tired or frustrated moment throw those resolutions to the wind and overcommit ourselves at work. Does that mean that it is useless to reset our objectives? Certainly not.

To take an extreme example, I talk almost every week to men and women who had set high standards for sexual fidelity in marriage. But then in a moment of temptation they have weakened and succumbed. They are in my office because their guilt is ripping at their insides. They are whipping themselves for having fallen short of their ideal, and wonder if they should confess to their mates. I take their guilt very seriously and urge that they find the restoration available in God's forgiveness. (Ordinarily it is not best to ask forgiveness of their mate unless he or she already knows—that may relieve the offender's conscience, but it may also leave a permanent wound in their spouse.) Once that repentance and forgiveness is done, they must stop the self-flagellation and return to their goal of monogamy. Usually such an experience makes one much more compassionate and forgiving toward others who stumble, and that is good. But will it cause them to aim at a lower standard from then on? And are they now hypocrites if they hold to and even talk about fidelity as the ideal? Certainly not. Far better to have high ideals and to have failed than to have no morals and regularly and remorselessly betray someone you love.

Our reach will always exceed our grasp. Or at least it should. The time to worry is when you no longer look back and see resolutions you have not met—that is, when you have stopped dreaming and stopped working to improve your self-discipline.

2. Carefully track your progress.

The best way to implement a concrete plan of self-improvement is to write down your objectives, including subsets, then to keep an accurate record of your progress.

A magazine survey found that only 37% of the workers who responded had goals, 5% of whom had recorded them on paper. *Those who had put them in writing achieved 90% of their goals.* Ernest Hemingway, who in many ways eschewed discipline, forced himself to write early every morning ("I don't think I've missed a sunrise in my adult life," he once said.) and recorded the number of words he completed each day. He used a wall graph to chart his daily output, and at the end of the day that number either encouraged him or scolded him. Management theorists have an axiom: "You can't change it until you can measure it," and that technique works as well for running your life as for running a large corporation.

Insurance salesman Harvey Cook is even more detailed than Hemingway in his recordkeeping. Harvey is an unassuming man in Phoenix, Arizona, who year after year is the most productive representative in the history of the mammoth Metropolitan Life Insurance Company. He has become so efficient that he can remain one of the company's top sales representatives even though he works only two days a week, seven months a year.

How has he done it? By setting daily, weekly, and yearly objectives for himself, building in a series of rewards, then keeping detailed records of his progress. Here is how he describes his plan:

To do what I do, I work two intense days. I plot out my week carefully, with the goal of completing thirty appointments in two days. I always carry with me a card with my plan for the day, and another I call the Score Card. If the goal is to make five presentations in the morning, and I accomplish that, I reward myself with lunch. If I don't get those calls in, I go without lunch. By the end of the evening, I need—according to my plan—to have made seven sales, and I keep going into the night until those are completed. If I get them done early enough, I can go home and enjoy an evening with the kids. Those goals—lunch, an evening with the kids—are before me all day, and the Score Card tells me exactly where I stand. My wife knows the figures also. She knows that if I'm on target, we can use the other five days to go flying, or drive up to our mountain cabin.

Three things are significant about Cook's method: (1) he builds in intermediate rewards as he goes along, (2) careful records make his incentive plan possible, and (3) though he works some intense hours, balancing time with his family is a part of his plan. Harvey has seven children to whom he is devoted and though he may not record the hours spent with his loved ones in quite the same detail as his sales calls, one does not have to be around him long to note that he pays a great deal of attention to how well his life stays in balance.

One thing is certain. If at the office we track carefully our day-to-day objectives and improve our efficiency, it will make us easier to live with in the evenings. As a friend's teacher wisely commented, "It is not the work you do that tires you, but work you leave undone."

To digress a bit, there is a fourth habit of Cook's worth noting: he allows himself some vacations from rigid self-discipline. He puts in highly regimented days, followed by periods when he can do what he wants. In order to maintain strong self-discipline in some areas, most of us find it necessary to have spots where we are unfettered. A prolific scholar I know works in the midst of the most astonishing clutter. He wastes time trying to find a book or an article in the stacks of material that cover almost every square foot of his office rug. But when it comes to his writing, he is a model of concentration and self-discipline. He works steadily, without turning to the right or left, as if he has blinders on. All morning. Five days a week. And his writing is as clear and pristine as his office is cluttered. I once asked him why he doesn't keep his notes and research material filed in some semblance of order. He looked around and said, "It *is* such a mess, isn't it? But I have the choice of spending the day organizing these books and papers, or spending five hours writing. And it's the writing that counts."

Perhaps there is more to it than that. To have areas where this man is quite disciplined, he probably needs to give his psyche the liberty to be untrammeled in other areas.

I do not want to overpromise or oversimplify here: merely having clear-cut goals and tracking them carefully will not assure your achieving success. Many people with high motivation and clear objectives don't make it to the top. But we can say that almost without exception no one gets there *without* these ingredients.

3. Build up a tolerance for pain.

When a new patient comes to me for psychotherapy, my first task is to make an assessment as to whether the person has a problem with which I can help. The second question I must answer is: Will this man or woman be willing to pay the price to change? Because, as I tell patients during the first session, if they are going to get their money's worth, they will leave my office some days feeling worse instead of better. Psychotherapy is akin to surgery. We must probe into sensitive areas, and the probing can hurt. When you awake in the recovery room after surgery, you feel sicker than when you went in, but the goal is that you return to health.

To cling to the belief that a pain-free life equals happiness actually diminishes our prospects for genuine happiness. More times than not the path that leads to fulfillment will contain some sacrifice. When you fear hardship, you miss out on the very endeavors that are the source of happiness: marriage, raising children, professional stature, religious commitment, sports achievements, self-improvement. Gary Player, who won more international golf tournaments in his time than anyone, was evidently tired one day when a spectator said, "I'd give anything if I could hit a golf ball like you," because Player's usual politeness failed him. He said:

No, you wouldn't. You'd give anything to hit a golf ball like me if it was easy. Do you know what you've got to do to hit a golf ball like me? You've got to get up at five o'clock in the morning, go out on the course, and hit one thousand golf balls. Your hand starts bleeding, and you walk up to the clubhouse, wash the blood off and slap a bandage on your hand, and go out and hit another one thousand golf balls. That's what it takes to hit a golf ball like me.

The tortoises of this world seem to assume that a second wind awaits them if they push long enough against personal discomfort. Although medical researchers say there is no such physiological phenomenon as the second wind, many of us have crossed a threshold of pain, then discovered a new spurt of energy on the other side. If this is a mental experience rather than a physical one, then even wider ramifications present themselves. When you learn that you can hang on longer than you thought possible in one situation, that makes it possible to persevere in other situations as well. You are acquiring power habits that will stand you in good stead for a lifetime.

The mountain climber's or athlete's embrace of pain for later glory is difficult for some to appreciate. Perhaps the principle is more understandable when we look at what women experience in childbirth, where pain turns into ecstasy. Physician Grantly Dick-Read wrote: "Young mothers with no pretensions to piety have unhesitatingly told me that at the birth of their child they felt the nearness of God, or the presence of a superhuman being, or a heavenly feeling that they have never known before." Pain, such as torture inflicted upon prisoners, is one thing. But pain with a constructive purpose—excelling at your craft, or bringing a baby into the world—is in a different category.

When Self-Discipline Gets Excessive

Before leaving the topic of pain, I must offer three disclaimers. The first is that deferred gratification is not the same as self-punishment. It is a mistake to suppose that self-discipline is learning to "conquer yourself." Rather, it is realizing that we are a bundle of contradictory impulses. The impulse to achieve coexists with the impulse to seek the easy way out; the impulse to become highly proficient in some field coexists with the impulse to pamper ourselves. When you decide to learn self-discipline, you decide to become unified. You are saying No to the self-indulgent and self-coddling tendencies, and Yes to the desire for accomplishment and self-mastery.

When Jesus urged his disciples to take the narrow gate and hard way, or when St. Paul talked about the virtue of self-control, these passages may appear on the surface to be contrary to healthy self-esteem. But they are just the opposite. Jesus and Paul are not asking us to become masochists who spend our lives on a bed of nails to show how much punishment we can endure. Rather, they are calling us to learn freedom and self-confidence through discipline.

Second, one can go overboard and defer gratification too long. I wish to emphasize that we are talking about *postponing* gratification, not forgoing it. Everyone has a story about some couple who rigorously saved their money and became so calcified in their thrift that they could never enjoy the money they'd saved. Or workaholics who kept their noses to the grindstone so long that they could experience pleasure only while working. Such people do not understand the principle of the harvest—that you invest now in order to reap dividends later. Workaholics cannot celebrate when the harvest comes in. Their only satisfaction is in what precedes it: plowing, sowing, weeding. These men and women love to make money and accumulate wealth, but rather than enjoying the fruits of their labor, they must immediately move on to gathering more.

Another problem for workaholics is that there is no balance for them *during* the pursuit—they furiously throw themselves into a schedule of unrelenting work and have no time for anything else. The work-now-play-later philosophy is basically sound but it is distorted badly when you never find time to play with the people you love or to take time to do something you enjoy doing, simply for the pleasure of it.

So our goal should be to enjoy the journey as well as the destination. Studies of painters have shown that if they are working only for fame or financial gain and do not enjoy painting they will never be great. Eugene Iso, the concert pianist and teacher of pianists, said a very similar thing. When he and his wife (the widow of his old friend, cellist Pablo Casals) were being interviewed, the conversation turned to what it takes to become a concert pianist. "If you do it with the goal of becoming famous, then don't try it," said Iso. "You must be willing to be unrecognized, and then you do it for the music itself." If you embark on a musical career knowing that you might end up repeating all the major and minor scales two hundred thousand times, it would be unbearable if you hated to practice and enjoyed only the public performances.

John Howard became the world's fastest self-propelled human being at the age of thirty-seven, when in the desert heat of the Bonneville Salt Flats, on July 19, 1985, he rode a bicycle at more than 152 miles per hour. Howard had competed in three Olympics and won a gold medal at the 1971 Pam Am games, but he was tossed off the Olympic team at age thirty because he was "too old." So he went out and won the Ironman Triathlon in 1981, set a world endurance record (riding a bike 512 miles in twenty-four hours) in 1983, and then began a two-and-a-half-year effort to break the speed record. For Howard, as for most people who dwell in the rarefied air of working very near to the limits of human capacity, his technique is driven by love and desire. "For any of this to make sense, you have to love the activity itself," he reports. "If you look on it as competition, if you look on it as work, you won't get anywhere. You have to appreciate what the bicycle can do for you; you have to look forward to your training runs, to the blue sky and the fresh air. You have to find gut-level enjoyment in the act itself. I learned that lesson. I used to work. Now I play."

4. Engage in a lifelong battle with procrastination.

If we are procrastinators, it not only infuriates supervisors and coworkers, it also botches up relationships with other important people. Why do some of us so readily fall into this trap? We procrastinate either because we are perfectionists and cannot bear to have our signature on anything with flaws. Or we procrastinate because of a distaste for difficult tasks and thus fill our time with less important work.

But those are not the reasons we usually give. We use several justifications to disguise this simple desire to avoid failure or difficulty.

"If I Put It Off, the Problem Might Go Away"

There is a faint possibility this could turn out to be true. Some problems do self-correct and occasionally projects get canceled or supervisors are transferred. But more commonly, other people will do the job if we wait long enough. Someone else will carry out the garbage; the sale can go to a competitor; the roof you were going to repair becomes irreparable; or your manager will give up and hand the assignment to another employee.

"I Always Do My Best Work Under Pressure"

Again, a grain of truth resides here. Most of us have discovered that we can accomplish more than usual when close to a deadline. But last-minute work is often sloppy work, and we frequently find that when working in a frenzy we did not allow enough time, or did not have the materials we needed, and we miss the deadline. (Douglas Adams once said: "What I love most about deadlines is the whooshing sound as they go by.")

"I Could Get Hurt Here"

Another justification for postponing difficult projects is our fear of rejection, though again, that is not often the reason we give. Children of demanding parents postpone finishing a job because they want to please their parents and are afraid of disapproval. Sales professionals procrastinate picking up the phone to make prospect calls because they know they will be turned down more often than they will turn up a prospect. We keep polishing a report past the deadline for fear of our supervisor's criticisms. As a result, our personal power is being throttled down by dread.

How do you counter these rationalizations and break the habit of procrastination? With constant vigilance. By pointing out to yourself the foolishness of your justifications when they arise and by deliberately forcing yourself to do things early. If you are always a last-minute person, and habitually get your taxes mailed just before midnight on April 15, do them in February. If your school papers are always late, start turning them in a week ahead. Those who avoid the traps of procrastination refrain from prolonging a difficult project. They take on as much as possible as early as possible, concentrate on it until it is finished, then the remainder of the week is far more enjoyable. As a bonus, they become known as a person who "gets things done."

Dianna Booher, in her book *Get a Life Without Sacrificing Your Career*, says, "If you're stuck on a project . . . start with the most dreaded part so you can get it over with. Then being over that biggest hump, you'll gain energy for the rest." I disagree. If you are a procrastinator by nature and must tackle the hardest part first, you could find yourself even *more* paralyzed. If so, then do the opposite of what Booher suggests: begin with some small, easy section of the project, then gradually chip away at it. Henry Ford once said that any problem, no matter how difficult, is solvable if you break it down into small, manageable parts.

When my clients fear a task because of possible failure or rejection, they often find that it helps to keep their eyes on past successes. For instance, if you have overcome major obstacles in the past, you may want to carry with you some token that reminds you of that triumph. An executive I know says that she can get blocked before making calls on delinquent accounts. So she carries a medal her company gave her for an outstanding year. "As soon as I get someone on the phone," she says, "I take that medal out of my desk drawer and hold it in my hand to remind myself that I'm good at what I do. It's surprising how a little thing like that can help you fight procrastination."

5. Beware the dangers of luxury.

Prosperity turns some people soft. In their early years they harden themselves to pain and exercise discipline. Then, as a result of the ensuing success, they find themselves enjoying comfort and luxury, wherein lurk some grave dangers. Ease and prosperity can eat away at our powers. Little by little, we become accustomed to the fat life and our old, lean toughness is gradually destroyed before we know what has happened. When we wake up, we discover that we have become less productive, that younger people have passed us up, and that much of our old muscle is gone.

Jesus inveighed strongly against the dangers of riches. Although I do not understand him to say that wealth itself is wrong, we know he is speaking the truth, because material prosperity and excessive luxury are always dangerous. Few people become more creative and alive when catapulted into a life of luxury, but we've all known men and women who were damaged or destroyed by it.

Those who cultivate psychological hardiness resist such dangers by holding on to the Spartan within. Fortune is always fickle, and if their fortunes change—if they are demoted, if their careers go into eclipse, or if they have to adjust their standard of living downward, they do not grumble. In fact, they almost seem to enjoy digging down and plowing hard as they did in the old days, because they find their old powers returning.

Rembrandt was the most popular painter of his day until he was about thirty-five. He had the whole of Holland—virtually the whole of Europe—applauding him, clamoring for his work. Then another painter appeared. Van Dyke was more elegant than Rembrandt, easier for the general public to grasp and understand, and Rembrandt's work was rejected in favor of the simpler work of his successor. Ten years before his death, Rembrandt was forced to sell everything he had, and he lived the last years of his life in poverty. And yet, he continued to paint furiously. According to one art critic, "Most of his finest painting belongs to those difficult years. . . . You cannot help feeling that the rejection had something to do with the greatness that followed; that the rejection, as it were, pierced him and struck open a new vein so that the genius was greater than ever."

6. Cultivate a strong sense of integrity and rigorously keep your promises.

"Every day, have some fun, make some money, and be ethical." That was the three-part directive given to one man on his first day on the job. Now president of his own company, he says that every time he hires someone new, he starts him or her out with that advice and tries to repeat it regularly.

The last piece of that counsel, on ethics and honesty, bears some examination, for it is an aspect of self-discipline that applies both to success at work and success at love. It is frequently remarked that honesty is always the best policy, but it is less frequently remarked that our integrity will frequently be judged not only by whether we relate facts accurately but also by how well we carry out our promises.

Two behavioral scientists, Morgan W. McCall, Jr. and Michael M. Lombardo, studied twenty-one executives who were fired. Their downfall was most often tied to a simple lack of trustworthiness. According to McCall and Lombardo, one of the indispensable traits for leaders is "a consistency and predictability built over time that says, 'I will do exactly what I say I will do when I say I will do it. If I change my mind, I will tell you well in advance so you will not be harmed by my actions.'"

A friend speculated at lunch recently that one could make a lot of money in a service industry—such as air conditioning repair or plumbing—by merely putting a large ad in the yellow pages saying: "We Show Up!" "It would be so startling to the average consumer to find such a company," the man contended, "that you could have more business than you could handle."

Two's Company Interiors designs and furnishes model homes for the building industry and does more than $2 million in business a year. The two women who started the company nineteen years ago know the importance of keeping a promise. Kathy Schroggie, one of the partners, says, "We've been able to survive the housing recession when our competitors were declaring bankruptcy left and right because we've never been late with an installation. Once, with a grand opening scheduled for the end of the week, and much of our furniture still on a truck somewhere between here and North Carolina, we went out and bought $5,000 worth of items at retail prices. That ate up most of our profit, but we couldn't let the builder down."

Samra Keller, president of West Venture Developers, their client on that project, verifies the value of such reliability: "When it comes to vendors, the best ability is dependability, and we'd stick with the women at Two's Company Interiors to our dying day when we know they'll go to such lengths to keep their word."

Truth-telling and reliability are also make-or-break virtues in our relationships outside of work. If our friends or our family discover that when in a jam we will say anything to wiggle out, or that we are inclined to overstate and exaggerate, their respect for us diminishes with every repetition of those habits. Moreover, if we are sloppy in keeping promises made to people we love, they gradually build up a knot of resentment. The best friends do not "forget" when they have promised a favor. And in the best families, people call when they're going to be late, they tell others about their changed plans, and when unable to carry through on an agreement, they let it be known well in advance. The strategy here for developing discipline is applicable both in business and in friendships: *Make few promises, then scramble like crazy to keep the ones you make.*

Wendell Will, an attorney in my town, prospered so well that he was able to retire a multimillionaire at age fifty. He once told me, "I'd like to think my success as a lawyer was due to my brilliant legal mind or my ability to sway a jury with spellbinding arguments. But I think it was really because I got things done pretty much when I said I would. If I told a client that a document would be ready at 10:00 a.m. on Friday, it was usually ready at about 10:00 a.m. on Friday. That quality is so rare today that if you have it, people think you're a genius."

PART THREE
COLLABORATION

6

ELICITING HELP
FROM OTHER
PEOPLE

"There is no such thing as a self-made person. You will reach your goals only with the help of others."

—GEORGE SHINN

IMBEDDED IN THE IDEA OF BALANCE IS A THIRD PRINCIPLE, the principle of collaboration: that no person is an island, that no one survives who tries to go too far alone, that two heads are almost always better than one, that joint ventures are necessary in order to thrive.

There will be many different levels of relationships, of course. At any given time we will have people at work— vendors, clients, perhaps supervisors—whom we cannot fully trust. It would be foolish to pretend otherwise. But highly effective people are always striving to establish better relationships with coworkers and more cooperative ventures with those who have abilities they do not have.

The same technique applies outside work: those with the best web of relationships constantly work to deepen their connections with friends and they enjoy the stimulus of meeting new people. All this is included in the important principle of collaboration. We grow and we accomplish the most in the company of loved ones, coworkers, colleagues, trusted advisors.

In their book, *When Smart People Fail*, Carole Hyatt and Linda Gottlieb listed nine reasons for career short circuits. Hands down, the single biggest one was what the researchers called "a lack of social intelligence." Most bright hard-working people who stumble for this reason never recognize the real cause. They often talk of "office politics" doing them in, but "office politics" is nothing more than interactions among people in the office; so if we have trouble there, we are really having trouble with our inter-personal skills.

Here is a secret about success in your career: you can get away with a considerable lack of talent and some unbelievable mistakes if you are socially intelligent. "This is the reason so many mediocre executives survive violent corporate upheavals," Hyatt and Gottlieb explain. "Sensitive in their dealings with others, these people are genuinely well liked, so when they make mistakes, their supporters help them recover."

High-achieving men and women have an uncanny way of making others want to help them. Their ability to understand human behavior, stimulate the people around them, and work smoothly with a variety of individuals makes them very much in demand. It can also multiply their salaries. John D. Rockefeller, Sr., once told Matthew C. Brush, "The ability to deal with people is as purchasable a commodity as sugar or coffee. And I will pay more for that ability than for any other under the sun."

Thick Networks

In order to thrive in almost every arena, one should build and maintain a strong set of contacts and friends—what professor John Kotter at Harvard Business School calls "thick networks." Think of several successful individuals you know. Isn't it true that they usually know by name far more people than most, and that they can quickly tap current telephone numbers for a bottomless group of people for almost anything they need? They stay in touch with school friends, call their old professors, talk to colleagues from former jobs, and maintain contact with a

They write twice as many Christmas cards as the average person.

diverse web of people that span various age groups over many organizational boundaries. They write twice as many Christmas cards as the average person and regularly send off notes and small gifts to their acquaintances.

Michael Korda, editor-in-chief at Simon and Schuster, says that by age forty you should have built a circle of friends in business—people who rely on you and to whom you can turn. These are colleagues for whom you do favors, whose projects you support, whose problems you listen to. And they do the same for you. John Stemmons, the legendary Dallas businessman, said a similar thing in a different way: "Find some people who are comers, who are going to be achievers in their own field, no matter what it is, and people you can trust. Then grow together." Many people spend an entire lifetime without discovering that principle. They assume that they had bad breaks or made unlucky career decisions, when in fact they could have succeeded if they had established themselves with a group of people who supported each others' undertakings.

Some individuals who get good reviews from their direct supervisors still fail in their organizations because they do not have enough support from people horizontally. In Warsaw not long ago, I had a chance to discuss with Polish managers and government leaders what the gurus of organizational dynamics theory call "matrix organizations": ones in which workers spend a great deal of their time working on teams with people not in their boss's chain of command. In matrix groups, you may not get regular performance reviews from the people sitting with you at the table, but you are making either positive or negative impressions of your ability. If you become known as a good collaborator and a catalytic influence in groups, you will almost certainly rise.

The Myth of the Solitary Genius

In her studies of Nobel laureates, Harriet Zuckerman found that the winners in science were much more likely than the average researcher to be collaborators and to coauthor their articles and books. Werner Heisenberg was at first an apprentice to Niels Bohr, but the two went on to collaborate together and hammer out the basis for modern quantum theory. British microbiologist James Watson, trying to break the genetic code, realized that he possessed too narrow a range of skills for the task and enlisted the help of physicist Francis Crick and x-ray crystallographer Maurice Wilkins, both of whom shared his fierce drive to win the race in which so many scientists were engaged. The three men won the Nobel Prize together.

Collaboration seems to have been at work frequently even in the so-called solitary arts, says John Briggs in his brilliant study of creativity, *Fire in the Crucible*. Picasso and Braque worked side by side to develop Cubism. Novelists Joseph Conrad and Ford Maddox Ford spent

> **Picasso and Braque worked side by side to develop Cubism.**

hours discussing the connotations of some word Conrad was considering for one of his stories, and Ford helped Conrad weather fits of exhaustion and despair. Unless you are a hermit in the Yukon, your ability to survive and succeed will depend heavily on your ability to form strong partnerships and alliances with people, and on your ability to multiply your efforts by working through others.

The Enormous Benefits from Having
Someone Who Believes in You

To accomplish something significant, you need at least one person who believes in your abilities, who encourages you to be creative, and who stands behind you if you decide to gamble with destiny.

One is fortunate if a parent or teacher shows such faith early on. When Steven Spielberg was a young boy in Arizona, his school days were not happy ones. "I was the last one picked for football, the last one picked for baseball, the last one picked for *badminton*," he said during an interview on CBS.

His mother, Leah, however, saw promise in him and encouraged his natural interests. "Steven always had a highly developed imagination," she says. Someone gave him a movie camera, and he began to come into his own. Leah often took him out of school and they would go into the desert with his camera. "We just had a ball," she says. Such a person who believes in you can push you a long way.

How One Book Became a Bestseller

Perhaps I can illustrate best the interconnections between success at work and success at love by describing Diane. Throughout the years when my writing was rejected, I never would have been able to persevere, had it not been for the determined optimism of my wife. There are stories of writers who paper their bathroom walls with rejection slips, and I accumulated enough for a very large bathroom. The manuscript for my first book was rejected by every major publisher in New York at least once (and in a few instances, twice, because I changed the title and sent it to different editors at the same firms). The bulky package would shoot back so quickly that I imagined publishers' offices to have whirling machines with a drum that sucked in piles of unsolicited manuscripts each day and sent them back out the door that evening with increased velocity.

As depressed and discouraged as I sometimes felt over those rejection letters, Diane never lost heart. She continued to believe in the book and did everything in her power to make it possible for me to keep writing. Eventually, Roland Seboldt, an editor in Minneapolis, liked what he read, and Augsburg Books printed it with the title *The Friendship Factor*.

About fifty-five thousand new books are published each year in the United States, which means that only a small fraction will even get into the bookstores. Because I was an unknown writer, and the publisher was not large, we knew we would have to promote the book in every way possible for it to have a chance. So I purchased the largest car-top carrier available and filled it with copies of the book. Diane and our two children set out on a six-week auto trip, stopping for any newspaper that would do an interview, or any service club that would allow me to give a speech. When the car-top carrier ran low, we would restock it along the way. This was hardly my children's idea of a vacation. If, say, we were in Tucson one night and I was due to speak at the Rotary Club in El Paso the next noon, it was necessary to get down the interstate at 4:00 a.m. While I spoke at the club and gave away a few copies of the book, my patient wife would entertain the children at some park.

Diane once asked how many copies the book would have to sell for it to be a success. I had heard somewhere that the publisher breaks even at about ten thousand copies, and since I was determined that the people who gambled on this project would not lose money, I told her that if it sold ten thousand, I'd be deliriously happy.

To date, *The Friendship Factor* is in more than fifteen languages, has gone through forty-nine printings, and has sold a million and a half copies. I'm not under any illusion that this is The Great American Masterpiece—no one knows why some books take off and others do not. But it never would have been published and never would have gained legs, had it not been for Diane's enthusiasm for the project. She is the light of my life.

None of us can stand too much rejection alone. One against the many is very hard. But two against the many! That's a different matter. You can go for years on such energy.

Many husbands and wives have built what John Briggs calls "domestic collaboration," that is, alliances with a mate who may not be directly involved in the creative work but provides a supportive environment in which the work can take place. A few men have provided such advocacy for their wives in the past, and in the twenty-first century, when women come into their own, many more men will have the opportunity. Among other things, we men in two-career families must assume more responsibility for keeping the home running smoothly. Too often our attitude is, "You can have a job and work as many hours as you need to, as long as you continue to clean, cook, do the laundry and all the other things women are supposed to do." For a man to take on many of these chores not only makes his wife's schedule more tolerable, it makes an important, bolstering statement about the value he places on her efforts to succeed in her vocation.

> "We human beings can survive the most difficult of circumstances if we are not forced to stand alone."
> —James Dobson, What Wives Wish Their Husbands Knew about Women

Virginia Woolf's husband, Leonard, commented on her writing and suggested changes, then helped keep her on an even keel through her emotional crises. Twenty-three years older than Georgia O'Keeffe, the famous photographer Alfred Stieglitz took the young woman under his wing because he admired her work. "What would you like to do?" he asked her shortly after she showed up at his studio in New York. "I'd like to go on painting," she replied.

"I will make that possible," said Stieglitz, and he did just that. Their marriage became a locus of energy and creativity for the art of both.

One need not be married to find such "domestic collaboration." Theo van Gogh was not an artist, but he had confidence in his brother, Vincent, and supported him when no one else would buy his paintings. (When Vincent van Gogh died in 1890 he had sold only one painting, for a paltry sum. Recently, van Gogh's "Portrait of Dr. Gachet" was auctioned for $82.5 million, a record for any sale of any painting.)

Such examples show that collaboration may take many forms but is an indispensable ingredient for good work.

The Traits of Good Collaborators

What is it in some people that causes others to want to help them and to enjoy working with them? And on the other hand, why do others have so much difficulty working with groups, both as participant and leader? Those questions are as complicated as the question of why we like some people and not others. But of this we can be certain: good leaders employ certain motivational principles to elicit loyalty. Herewith, then, some characteristics of leaders who know how to create in others a desire to help them.

They are straightforward in asking for help.

It is remarkable what you can accomplish if you're not afraid to ask for assistance. Eldon Holl, a CPA who spends much of his time testifying in court as an expert witness, once told me how he achieved his knowledge. "I learned a long time ago," he replied, "to pick up the phone when I needed to get up to speed on some topic. You can call people renowned for their expertise, and say, 'I want to buy a couple of hours of your time. I'm a newcomer to this field and need to get educated.' Almost everyone—no matter how famous or important—will say, 'Sure, come on over.' Sometimes they send me a bill (which I am glad to pay), but more often, they not only give their time at no charge, they also call later with some article they clipped or some further piece of advice. Sometimes they became important business associates and allies."

Why do we so often hesitate to ask for help? Perhaps because we fear exposing our ignorance or we think others will flaunt their superiority when we need assistance. But we should realize that we actually do them a favor. Few acts are so gratifying as assisting some newcomer in one's field, and rather than looking down on you when they've helped you, most people will have a strong affinity for you. Especially if you have a position over them, such as supervisor, teacher, or parent. They now have an investment in you and want to see you succeed. The great general and military strategist George C. Marshall once said, "If you want a man to be for you, never let him feel he is dependent on you. Make him feel you are in some way dependent on him."

Just how should one go about asking for help? "Never claim as a right what you can ask as a favor," someone once told me. You can issue orders to employees or children. Or you can say, "I need to ask a favor." The latter approach puts the relationship on an entirely different level.

Example. Your family has financial difficulties. Some parents—especially fathers—consider money troubles the last thing to talk over with the family. But your children are fully capable of pitching in. Rather than yelling, "What this family needs to do is learn that money doesn't grow on trees," it is better to say, "We're in a cash crunch right now and need to tighten our belts for a while, so I'd like to ask for your help. When you see ways you think we could save money, could you let us know? If you see lights not being used, please turn them off, and if there are other ways we can reduce our spending, please give us your best thinking." That little speech will work equally well if you're asking a family to reduce its spending by $1,000 a year, or if you're requesting your staff to cut its budget by $10 million.

Asking for help also cements friendships. Let's say that you are single, you live alone, and things have gone crossways with a coworker. You can't discuss it with anyone on the job, it's 1:00 a.m., and you can't sleep for stewing over the problem. What to do? Hopefully you have a network of friends among whom the agreement is that you can call each other at any time of the day or night. Choosing one, you call and say, "I'm sorry about the hour, but I need your help. For some reason I'm getting myself into a state about a problem at work, and I need a little advice before I do something stupid tomorrow. Would you mind meeting me for a cup of coffee?"

Unless you abuse these privileges that accompany the best friendships, your friend will be honored by the request and will get to the coffee shop before you do. In talking with my patients, I sometimes suggest that to cut down on their psychiatric bill they take such an action when they are in trouble. They usually respond, "I could never do that! I don't care how good the friend, I wouldn't call in the middle of the night."

"OK, turn the situation around," I reply. "Think of one of your two or three best friends. If that person called you at 2:00 a.m. and asked for your help, would you feel imposed upon?"

Usually they think a moment and reply, "Well no, of course not. I would feel good to be needed like that."

They take an optimistic view toward people.

Whether others will want to help you in various enterprises and assist you in keeping your life in balance will depend more on your attitudes than on any specific psychological techniques you employ. In our survey of men and women who excelled in their careers, my colleagues and I often asked them their "secrets." The best leaders would often say, "Oh, I don't have any secrets, except that we have a lot of good people here."

When you like people and have a genuine concern for their well-being, they sense that very quickly. On the other hand, when you take a callous view of workers as if they were mere units of energy, or treat your children or friends as if they were property, that becomes clear as well. If you have enough power, your underlings may not talk back to you but they will torpedo your plans at the earliest opportunity.

In our research we found, quite to our surprise, that those who elicited the strongest loyalty almost never possessed "charisma." Robert Wodfruff is a good example. He was president of Coca-Cola for thirty-two years and the person most analysts regard as responsible for the company's growth into a multinational, worldwide giant. It was his positive attitude toward people and his capacity for selecting and developing staff that distinguished him. Someone described Woodruff as "not very exceptional . . . other than his exceptional success." A later president of Coca-Cola said: "Bob has no particular talents. He's not a technical man or an advertising man. He is fumbling in his talk. . . . But he has an ability for finding good people and for binding them to him, for developing in them an extraordinarily deep sense of loyalty. I am dedicated to Woodruff as to no other man alive."

They rely on the mentoring system.

In our survey, we were also surprised to find that so many prominent men and women attributed their achievement to early teachers. Perhaps their business models had long since retired, perhaps they were no longer living, yet when

I interviewed successful people, these mentors continued to be an inspiration. Sometimes pictures of predecessors hung in the office somewhere, and I would hear things like, "Everything I learned about running this company I learned by watching Charlie."

This finding from our interviews is corroborated by research published in *Harvard Business Review*. In a survey of nearly four thousand executives who performed unusually well, Gerald R. Roche found that fully two-thirds of the respondents had mentors. The managers with mentors were better educated, earned more money at a younger age, and were happier in their work than those who had never had such sponsors.

Anyone who ever hopes to achieve the level of mastery in the martial arts, music, or dance, studies with a master. To be a good athlete requires two things: both talent and drive. But to be a world-class athlete there is yet a third requirement: a world-class coach. Sometimes it is not easy to find the best teachers in your field and you may have to try several before finding the true master. But once you have located such a person, it is worth walking fifty miles each week to study there.

Successful people not only give credit to early mentors in business but also to parents and extended family who taught them certain fundamental habits and ways of approaching problems. One man told us that his father had definite ideas about how to teach youngsters to work. "My dad didn't believe fathers were in a position to demonstrate to their children how manager-employee relations worked. I grew up on a farm, and when I was a little boy I helped Dad at home. But when I was older, he always arranged for me to get summer jobs with some uncle or relative whom he admired. They all lived nearby. One operated a food processing plant, others had farms much like ours. But when I worked for an uncle, the job was on a different level. Like their employees, I had to arrive on time every morning and work hard all day. But also like them, I received a check every week, with overtime pay and deductions. This extended family—these uncles whom I'd hunted with and looked up to—taught me a lot about the value of sweat, about having fun on the job, and about principles of problem solving."

It is a wise executive who promotes the mentor system among workers. If you can get the veterans in your office, who may have millions of dollars' worth of experience and skill, to motivate and teach newcomers, it can make your job much easier. Sometimes the veterans will hesitate to reveal their secrets for fear of being replaced. But if you reward rather than punish your people for the hours they spend teaching others, they will do it happily, for there is scarcely a person alive who does not get fulfillment from taking another person under wing.

They learn to share power with others.

Here is a curious phenomenon: some loners do well in the early stages of their careers. They master their specialty and rise rapidly because they are competitive and hard-driving. But then they begin to stall, and the reason is confusing. They continue to work hard, but others are surpassing them. How does this happen?

In a fascinating article, "The Derailment of Fast-Track Managers," Barbara E. Rovach says many of the whiz kids who fizzle do so because they fail to make the transition from specialist to generalist: they do not learn to share power with others. It is not surprising that they miss this fork in the road, for it requires almost forsaking the skills that put them ahead early in their careers. Rovach, a professor of management at Rutgers University, writes:

> In the early years of the career . . . the fast-trackers
> as a whole are individualistic and achievement

oriented, focusing on what they themselves can accomplish through their own efforts. Much of this must be forgotten in the mid-years of the careers . . . when the transition from individual to group achievement, from solo flights to partnership, and from competition to cooperation must be learned. Then in the senior years [one must create] an environment in which *many others* can achieve, and where the measure of one's own work is, in fact, the measure of the work of others.

If you can move from mastering your specialty to mastering the art of management and motivation, the sky's the limit. Another way to say this is that if we are to advance we must learn to delegate. Many people cannot or will not do this. They make assignments, then when the project gets into trouble, they re-involve themselves, inwardly enjoying the role of rescuer but outwardly complaining about their hours and how you can't get good help. Such people make very exasperating leaders. The competitive urge is still so strong in them that they must prove their superior ability to the employees. And indeed they probably *are* better at many tasks. But it is a foolish way to lead, and leaves a staff demoralized. "Delegation is half of success," says Michael Korda. "People who cannot delegate will find themselves fatally handicapped. By the time you reach forty, you'd better be an expert at it, which means you have to pick the right people and trust them."

Does this principle apply in developing good families and maintaining a life in balance? Indeed it does. If you take a collaborative approach to work at home, it makes for a much better family. Some harried mothers and fathers say, "I have tried giving my kids chores but it hasn't made for a happy family at all. The children complain so loudly and do things so poorly that it's easier to do it myself."

Of course it is. At least the first time, perhaps the third and fourth times. Perhaps even the twentieth time. But you do your children no favors by allowing them to live in a group where they do not share some of the work. They thrive by learning the value of good labor. They learn discipline. And eventually they learn how to do certain tasks well. When there is division of labor and delegation of responsibilities, your children will be better off, your house will run more smoothly, and you will be able to keep your own life more balanced.

They consider it a major goal to help people below them grow.

Earlier, we discussed how people who achieve a high state of excellence in their craft usually begin with mentors. If the process works correctly, you will move out from under the tutelage of your mentor (and that can be a little traumatic for both teacher and student), then begin coaching younger people who are on the way up. If you take such an approach, those on your team will remain exceedingly loyal.

This principle of leaders training leaders was employed by Moses as he led the Children of Israel, and it certainly was Jesus' method. He, like all of us, had only a finite number of hours in each day. It puzzled some observers at the time that Jesus often passed up opportunities for speaking and healing where crowds would be present. What did he choose to do instead? He trained a small band of people—a dozen men who would grow in their understanding of faith and eventually turn the world upside down. All persons who head large organizations and still have time to balance their lives with friends and loved ones do that: they help some people around them grow, get those men and women to do some of their work for them, then watch them soar.

I knew a sales manager who had under him almost a thousand realtors who produced $3 billion in sales every year. He told me, "Some superb salespeople make terrible sales managers because they are by nature impatient. They often are the types who say, 'lets-find-a-way-to-make-the-deal-today.' That's good for selling, bad for managing. I think I've been good at leadership because I know it takes time to develop people. Before getting into this work I coached high-school football. I like to see others grow."

It is a fascinating concept of the leader: not so much as general but as coach. It is also an important metaphor for parents to contemplate because with our children we must at times be a dictatorial general, at times teacher, and at other times a combination of both. When our children are young, the authoritarian approach is frequently necessary ("Don't touch the hot pan; it'll burn you." "It's time to put your shoes on.") But later, in what George Valliant calls "the passing on of wisdom," we stop exercising raw power and shift to the role of coach or mentor, when we pass on wisdom and values not so much by coercion as by persuasion.

This can happen during one-on-one contact. It happens when parents read Bible stories that impart some moral principle to their young children. It happens when the family is driving in the car and a mother or father ruminates about some difficult decision at work that offered the opportunity to cheat and improve profits, or to do what was right. It happens when the family as a whole takes on some act of unselfishness and compassion for those less fortunate—the project may be inviting someone in trouble to stay in their home for a few weeks, sending money each month to support an orphan in Rwanda, or volunteering as a family to help in a soup kitchen once a week. These are the ways values are formed.

When success occurs, they share the credit and rewards with others.

In almost every in-depth study of achievement, the

researchers found that people at the top were lavish in giving praise to their spouses and family. This was true of a survey of British chief executives. It was true of the Grant Study, a fifty-year longitudinal study of 268 men now supervised by George Valliant at Harvard. And my colleagues and I certainly found it to be true among the more than 300 men and women whom we interviewed in our informal survey. They never pretended that they could have succeeded alone. They liked to tell about people, such as relatives, who loaned them the money to begin their businesses, and they talked about the encouragement of friends. They told us that there had been days when they could not have endured had it not been for the secure cocoon called home to which they would be retreating that evening.

Not only do those who succeed give credit to their families and mentors. Almost without exception they give credit to their colleagues and coworkers as well. At first it may sound like false modesty when effective business executives say that their secret is having "good people" in their organizations; yet it is clear that without discounting their roles as vision setters, decision makers, motivators, and referees, these leaders believe they move ahead in their careers because of the talented individuals with whom they work.

Good managers always look for ways to build in more incentives for their staff members. The message is: everyone is crucial to the success of this organization, and if we all pitch in and work together well so the company does well, we'll all be rewarded. It is an old axiom first stated by Andrew Carnegie: "The easiest way to get rich is by enriching others."

Dr. Franklin Murphy, who excelled at a remarkably wide variety of enterprises—physician, University of Kansas Medical School dean, UCLA chancellor, chairman of Times-Mirror Corporation—was obviously a brilliant man with

wide-ranging talents. Yet he made an extraordinary claim
about his technique for getting things done:

> The people around me have made me successful. I
> would never have been able to accomplish any-
> thing on my own. I have always sought out people
> who I felt were talented, who had self-discipline. I
> then tried to develop their affection and loyalty. I
> have recruited them, motivated them, and when we
> were able to achieve something, I shared the credit
> with them.

7

THE CHARACTERISTICS OF HIGH-MORALE TEAMS

"Management is, all things considered, the most creative of all arts. It is the art of arts. Because it is the organization of talent."

—Jean-Jacques Serran-Schreiber

"Our landings . . . have failed . . . and I have withdrawn the troops," wrote General Dwight Eisenhower, Supreme Commander of the Allied Forces, as he sat at his portable table, carefully writing out a press release in longhand. The date was June 5, 1944. "My decision to attack at this time and place was based upon the best information available," he went on. "The troops, the air and the Navy did all that bravery and devotion to duty could do. If any blame or fault attaches to the attempt, it is mine alone." Eisenhower folded the paper, put it in his wallet to be used in case the invasion failed, and went to dinner.

In many ways, Eisenhower had been an unlikely choice for supreme commander of the largest military force ever amassed in the history of civilization. Growing up poor in Kansas and Texas, Eisenhower had been able to get an appointment at West Point, where he was well-liked but not a star student—in a class of 164, he was 61st in academics and 125th in discipline. By 1940, an obscure lieutenant colonel at Fort Lewis, he had been in the Army twenty-eight years without seeing combat.

In order to prevail, this untested American would have to forge a smooth military force from several nations, all with different traditions and different objectives, and he must build a leadership team comprised of such eccentric and exasperating leaders as Winston Churchill, George Patton, Charles de Gaulle, and George Montgomery. (Even Churchill once said of Montgomery, "He was magnificent in defeat and insufferable in victory.") It was small wonder, then, that when this untested American arrived in London, war-weary England was wary.

Although D Day, 1944, was a great gamble, Eisenhower never had to release his statement explaining the invasion's failure. By the next evening, the world learned that in a twenty-four-hour period, the air forces had flown 10,500 sorties, 23,000 airborne troops had been dropped into Normandy at night, and 132,715 British, American, and Canadian troops had gone ashore during the day.

Hitler's much-touted Atlantic Wall had been breached.

Why was Eisenhower successful? Because, despite his modest record and the fact that some of his generals could spot him by ten or twenty IQ points, he had an unusual blend of talents. He knew how to construct a coalition, then even-handedly push, persuade, cajole, and mollify its various elements until it became a well-oiled machine.

It is an art that will be essential for accomplishment in the twenty-first century and for the constructing of a well-rounded life. While at times being asked to work alone, we will also find ourselves increasingly interdependent, and to excel we must be able to assemble and manage cooperative ventures.

The Power of the Affiliative Motive

Effective leaders understand how to tap into the great need everyone has to be a part of some group. We were not built to function well alone, and particularly in this time, with its dislocations, its isolations, and its structures that make for loneliness, people are desperate for community. Why have gangs grown so rapidly in our cities? Because with the destabilization of the family, young people must have some group where they know people will be loyal to each other. They are willing to risk imprisonment or even their lives for it. The need for community is simply that powerful.

Anyone who has been in a combat zone knows that soldiers are never motivated to fight out of pure patriotism. Nor do they risk their lives because of hatred for the enemy or nationalistic fervor. When you must actually do battle, you have only two motives: you hope to stay alive and you want to help your buddies. Psychologists have called the second "the affiliative motive." That is, most of us will pay a large price to be a part of some group of people where we depend on each other—where we know that others will cover for us, stand up for us, and bail us out if we're in trouble. If you can create such an association, people will flock to join you, work harder than they've ever worked, and often stick with you even if the financial benefits would be greater in some other place.

Bear Bryant, football coach at the University of Alabama, in his pep talks before a game knew how to appeal to the best in his players. He would vividly paint for them a description of the hugs they would get from each other when the game was over, the smell of food at the banquet where the awards would be given out. He would say how much he thanked both his players and "the mothers and dads, girlfriends, high-school coaches, preachers," that had inspired them. It is a fascinating list, showing that Bear

Bryant knew a great deal about what motivated his players. Of course, they were motivated by the prizes at the end, but even more, they were motivated by the desire to hold each other up, and to make the people who were important to them happy.

The wise leader recognizes not only that everyone has a profound psychological need to belong to some group, but also that a peculiar power is operative when people link arms in a common cause. In the rooms where twelve-step meetings are conducted, one of the favorite quotations from the Bible is "Where two or three are gathered in my name, I am there among you." And indeed, millions of people have found that they can accomplish certain things—such as conquering alcoholism or drug addiction—in such company that they could never do alone. There is hardly any heightened experience that compares with what you feel when tightly connected with one or more persons for such a purpose.

How to Develop Group Spirit

Let us turn now to some specific characteristics of good group dynamics. High-morale teams operate best . . .

. . . When communication is valued.

Late one night in the stacks of Princeton's Firestone Library, I sleepily sifted through a pile of studies about notable people in England. In a book about the heads of British corporations, I was startled awake to find this statement: "When presidents of corporations were asked what personal characteristics they thought to be most important to their careers, hard work was not at the top, nor was intelligence. 'The ability to communicate,' headed the list." I read the sentence again. *The ability to communicate?* Who would have guessed? Perhaps the ability to get your ideas across is actually more important than talent or the number of hours you work.

Women may be a little better at such skills than men. A man who is head of an executive recruiting firm in Tulsa told me, "There was a time when the women who succeeded in business were tough and macho—like their male counterparts. But no longer. Now, with the command-and-control model out the window, they are appreciated for some of the wonderful feminine qualities with which they've either been born or which they've acquired (I'm not sure which it is, and it doesn't really matter), and one of those is their ability to communicate."

Women probably learn to articulate their thoughts and feelings in early childhood. Someone has commented that people used to look out on the playground and say that the boys were playing soccer and the girls were doing nothing. But the girls weren't doing nothing—they were talking. They were talking about the world to one another. And they became very expert about that in a way the boys did not.

Katie MacWilliams, a thirty-five-year-old head of a unit at First National Bank of Chicago that specializes in the arcane business of swapping commodity options, says fostering commitment in her twelve-person group is top priority: "You want them to come in and fight the good fight every day." Her strategy is hardly esoteric. Out of the morass of changing management theories, she has stuck with two fundamental lessons: "Keep 'em informed and get 'em involved." She consults with everyone who has a stake in her decisions—before she makes them.

Rapid growth requires stepped-up communication. When a business team or a family suddenly increases in size, the information flow needs to be increased correspondingly, for with each additional person, the number of relationships increases exponentially. In such periods of expansion, skilled leaders go to great lengths to find ways to keep everyone up-to-date. For instance, company newsletters are now increasingly obsolete. Progressive organizations are using email, faxes, and television monitors installed in offices and factories in order to trasmit information instantly. Unless leaders understand the value of such communication, news gets disseminated by the grapevine, and the grapevine is notoriously discriminatory. Someone always gets left out. And nothing is more demoralizing than to discover that everyone else knew something and you did not.

Perhaps people grow tired of family therapists saying so often that "lack of communication" is at the root of so many difficulties, but we say it frequently because we see in our offices the social havoc created by small misunderstandings that grow into a series of major short circuits. Good living arrangements exist when family members and roommates tell each other their plans and inquire regularly of each other's well-being. Small notes left on the kitchen counter telling where you are and when you'll be home, wishing a child good luck in a game, asking about arrangements for sharing cars—these are the day-to-day dialogues that make it possible for the activities of busy people to blend well and for love to flower.

It is one more example of the interconnections between work and outside relationships. Many people who fail in their careers—no, I would say that most people who fail in their careers—do so because of relational difficulties. So it follows that if you have learned good techniques for communicating outside work, you will be more effective in your vocation.

. . . When the group has fun together.

The wise manager resists the impulse to say, "Okay, it's time to stop having fun and get back to work," as if the two were inimical. Of course, if a project is behind schedule, or a team is slacking off, someone must crack the whip. But groups with good morale recognize that a certain amount of relaxation and frivolity is even *more* crucial when the group is under stress and working long hours. The wooden approach to this would be to plan an annual company picnic (especially if it is on the workers' time rather than the company's). But good leaders and good group members understand that laughter is essential throughout the working day, and that everyone can improve the mood by engaging in frequent banter with his or her associates.

"We still make each other laugh," said a woman in my office, and I quietly felt relief, for her marriage now looked less hopeless. Laughter and love are close relatives.

My friend, Murray Finck, who is now an effective executive, tells about growing up on a farm in Missouri. "My grandparents lived in the middle of the farm," he remembers, "and we lived down the road at one corner."

My uncle and aunt lived down the road on the other corner. It was a wonderful way for a little boy to grow up, being embraced and stimulated by all that family in close proximity.

If ever there was a man who balanced work and play, it was my grandfather. He worked very hard on the farm, but his pace and intent were distinctive, and I learned some important models from him. He was a very poetic kind of fellow. When we weren't in school, Grandpa liked to take some of us grandchildren out to the fields with him. One hot day we took a break under the shade of a huge hickory tree, leaning our backs against the trunk. Grandpa asked me to tell him all my sensations right then: what images the bark was imprinting on my back, what stories the old tree could tell, what I saw in the branches overhead, how far up I thought I could climb and what route I'd take.

When some grandchildren were accompanying him out to the field, Grandfather always threw a big rope and a board for a swing into the back of the pickup. He would eye the big trees that edged our farm until he found one near where he'd be working that was right, and he would throw the rope up over the limb and seemed to enjoy pushing us in big high swirls. Then he would watch us play while he did his work.

I asked Murray if he ever did that with his own children. He broke into a big smile and said, "Oh, yes. When I was a young father, I made a swing with a rope just like Grandpa's, and to this day, when we go on a picnic or to a park, I make certain the swing is in the trunk. Squinting up at the trees looking for a good limb, I think of Grandpa and my spirit lightens."

. . . When the individual never gets lost in the group.

Here is a paradox: While we all have a need to belong and like to be members of tight associations, we also have a need to protect our individuality. Good coalitions come together where the need for affiliation and the need for independence meet. It can be confusing to the leader when a group member displays both these instincts, but it is human nature for our employees or students to have such alternating feelings. No one wants to be merely a cog in the wheel, or a number on a time card, and group participants need to know that the leader notices their histories and particularities, their preferences and dislikes, their dreams and struggles.

Susanna Wesley, the mother of Charles and John Wesley, was also the mother of seventeen other children. From the vantage point of twenty-first century parent, we wonder, "How could any mother do right by all those kids? It was a challenge in the nineteenth century also, and one of the ways Mrs. Wesley solved it was by doing this: she made certain that she had an hour alone with each child every week. We don't know a great deal about that mother's weekly conversations with her little ones, but we can be sure of this: she understood them as individuals, not merely as parts of her brood.

Another way to say this is to say that in the best groups, diversity is welcomed. Now that we are working more on task forces and being encouraged to homogenize, creativity can get stifled. On the other hand, new ideas and good work occur in places where a certain amount of eccentricity is tolerated, where the people like each other, and where they feel that their ideas will be received with respect. According to one commentator, "the renewing corporations have plenty of wild ducks who may be several standard deviations off the cultural norm."

In the twenty-first century, the most effective leaders will be those who can bring disparate people together, and while allowing them to be themselves, help them find a common cause.

. . . When the group celebrates success.

A specific way to build fun into the workday (and one far more effective than the company picnic) is to celebrate your group's triumphs on the spot whenever possible. I notice that good families and good companies have parties at the drop of a hat. If a project comes in on time, the leader takes the group out for a long lunch and presents everyone with some small gift. Or a group of Little League parents get together for a potluck supper when they've reached their fund-raising goal. Even if you merely bring in a cake or show up with a box of milkshakes for your employees at the office, it can help the mood.

This principle applies as much for group members as much as for its leader. They need to recognize that the boss needs cheering up at times. So when he or she does something significant—especially if it was something on their behalf—celebrating that will mean more than they may realize. High-morale families go out to dinner when a child brings home a good report card, someone finishes a hard report, or a family member gets a raise, and they have frequent occasions when extended family and friends are invited in to commemorate some happy event or the anniversary of some success.

The act of breaking bread with another contains powerful symbolism, and meals have long been a vehicle for cementing friendships. I know two busy businessmen who talk on the phone regularly, but though they live and work in same city, they do not see each other often. They are careful, then, to remember each other's birthdays and for decades now have guarded those two lunches every year. Such rituals are bonds that hold us together.

. . . When the leader sets a vision.

In his sprightly book, *God, Country, and Notre Dame*, Father Theodore Hesburgh, who was president of Notre Dame through some of its greatest years (and not incidentally, through some of its best football seasons), says, "The very essence of leadership is that you have to have a vision. It's got to be a vision you articulate clearly and forcefully on every occasion. You cannot blow an uncertain trumpet."

Much in the current business fads with names like, "management by consensus," and "empowerment" is overstated. For instance, to assume that "participatory management" means that a group can function leaderless is errant nonsense. The fact of the matter is that some people are born to be followers, and the follower can become overwhelmed by problems rather than challenged by them. If the group has no guidance in thinking strategically, its members begin to fragment and mill about in confusion.

They need a visionary leader who sets a "can-do" tone and keeps the group moving into the future.

Henry Kissinger, describing French President Charles de Gaulle, said, "A great leader is not so much clever as lucid and clear-sighted. Grandeur is not simply physical power but strength reinforced by moral purpose." This is not necessarily an autocratic leader, but one who is unafraid to lead. This is the person who has a plan, who takes action even if the outcome is unclear, who is willing to stay out front where it is lonely, who is willing to make mistakes, who is able to look far beyond where others look and see dreams fulfilled.

In our examination of successful individuals, we found an unexpected common denominator in the way their minds worked. They had a knack for seeing the pattern in things. The philosopher Schopenhauer, commenting on the fact that certain people rise so high above the masses, said, "Always to see the general in the particular is the very foundation of greatness." And Russell Palmer, former dean of the Wharton School of business says, "The good leader is always a person who sees the big picture, and keeps focusing his or her organization on those major objectives, refusing to allow them to get bogged down with insignificant details."

. . . When everyone understands that certain things can be accomplished better alone.

Before giving a speech to a business group in Vancouver, Canada, not long ago, I talked with a manufacturing executive who, since we had last seen each other, had been promoted to a senior position in the corporate office in Toronto. He was not happy about being at this meeting, where he was to make a ten-minute presentation as part of a panel discussion. "To tell you the truth," he said, "I get frustrated with this team approach to everything. For instance, our whole group of vice presidents spent the day yesterday flying across Canada to this meeting, though most of us don't have any substantial contribution to make. We don't make decisions on our own, we just spend hundreds of hours reading email and sitting in meetings."

It was a legitimate complaint. Some of the most imaginative ideas and some of the best decisions come from people who have time to close the door and think. An understanding of a person's need for solitude (which varies a great deal with different individuals) means that in good families you are free to do things and go places alone without anyone feeling rejected. And it means that in the best work teams you do not try to do everything in the same room.

. . . When the leader is willing to step in to solve intramural feuds.

People function well on teams when they subordinate their personal feuds in order to win the battle. Anytime we hear a business leader or a parent say, "This conflict between you two is not my problem, it's yours, and you two have to iron it out," we can be certain that the group will eventually start to malfunction. There are times when managers (or parents, chairpersons, clergy) must step in, listen to both sides, decide on a compromise, then put all their weight behind the compromise. Choosing when to step into such situations and when to wait can be a difficult call, but when your group knows that you insist on their working together, it is more likely that they will try to resolve the dispute themselves.

On the one hand those who are the best collaborators are not afraid of fights, and on the other hand they expect to do some compromising and negotiating every day of their lives. I once sat in the office of a CEO who said, "Right now, my number one priority is working with two division heads who haven't been speaking to each other for a month. I've tried to figure out who started it and who's right and who's wrong, and it's pretty obscure. So we're not going to waste a lot of time on that. What I do is bring them into my office regularly and try to help them see each other's point of view. They're valuable well-meaning people, and I hope I don't have to lose one or both, but we can't tolerate this over any length of time."

A few months later, when we talked on the phone, I asked about the feud he'd been refereeing. "Oh, that?" he said. "It blew over, and now I'm ironing out some others. Good morale doesn't come easily, but we keep working at it here until it happens."

If a family is to be successful, it helps if its members have some understanding of why some groups split apart and why others stay together, and if at least one person, like my CEO friend, is dedicated to making the center hold. When divorces occur, I usually find that while the primary conflict may be between husband and wife, other grudges and rivalries—sometimes in the extended family—contribute to the fragmentation. This is especially true in blended families, with "your kids, my kids, and our kids." Left to their own devices, and without someone dedicated to smoothing out the feuds, the centrifugal forces at work in such groups can lead to terrible tragedies. But many of us have been fortunate to be in homes where people are committed to helping each other succeed at the art of love, committed to finding some common ground of compromise in times of difficulty, and committed to making the family work. As a sign on one mother's refrigerator door said, "So it's NOT home sweet home. Adjust!"

. . . When the group takes responsibility for quality.

The worst possible families and the worst possible companies are ones in which no one covers for anyone, where people shirk tasks by saying, "That's not my job," or "It's not my department."

The best possible groups are those where people take responsibility for quality and morale. When you see a piece of trash in the parking lot, you pick it up. Not because your job description calls for you to assist maintenance, but because you take pride in the way your facilities look.

A friend bought an old foundry a few years ago that required major modernization and cutting down the work force. "Among the people I inherited," he told me, "I found a group of old-timers in the machine shop who stayed to themselves, but who consistently turned out the best work in the plant, despite their antiquated equipment. I watched them closely and realized that when they got together to drink coffee, they would show each other their work, scoffing at something that was substandard and admiring what was good.

"It would have been a great mistake to split those men up, because not only did each one take pride in his individual work: there was also a strange peer pressure and group pride operating there as well. It seemed to be important to them that they not allow anyone in their group to fail. The consequence was that they all did better work because of the inner competition and loyalty." That foundry owner knew how to allow the group to do much of his supervision for him.

Here is an example of the same principle at work in a family. At a dinner meeting after a conference in Sun Valley, I sat next to a mother of six children, all of whom had distinguished themselves. They had graduated from schools like Stanford and Wellesley. There was not a bad apple among them. "How in the world did you motivate them?" I asked.

"Everyone asks me that," she laughed, "and the embarrassing thing is that I don't think I did much. I never told them to do their homework or scolded them when they made poor grades. They seemed to motivate one another naturally. For instance, I remember the day one of our daughters brought home a report card that was less than it should have been. I didn't say anything and put it back on the kitchen counter. When her older brother came home from school, he looked at it, snorted, then went to her room and gave her a big pep talk. I'm not sure exactly what he said, but among other things he convinced her that there were family standards she was supposed to maintain, and that if she didn't do her best, it would be a reflection on everyone in the family. It must have been some speech, because she dramatically raised her grades by the next report. She admired and loved her brother so much—she would have done anything to stay in his good graces."

That mother had done almost exactly what every good manager does: she had built a group-wide appreciation for excellence, then let the group itself take responsibility for its execution.

For many years, Max De Pree headed the Herman Miller Company, a Fortune 500 firm often referred to as "brilliantly managed." In his book, *Leadership Is an Art*, De Pree says that leadership is "more tribal than scientific, more a weaving of relationships than an amassing of information." Those who recognize the need for affiliation, and who build an environment where "tribal loyalties" are allowed to operate well, can look forward to some remarkable and rewarding outcomes—both in their work and in the web of connections with people outside their work.

8

TEN WAYS TO CRITICIZE WHILE KEEPING THE ATMOSPHERE POSITIVE

"If you ever run into an industry that says it needs better people, sell its shares. There are no better people. You have to use ordinary, everyday people and make them capable of doing the work."

—PETER DRUCKER

A BUSINESS CONSULTANT IS IN LINE TO CHECK HIS BAGGAGE at JFK Airport. The beefy man in front of him is abusive and impolite to the airline clerk, citing him and his airline with a list of grievances. Yet the airline clerk is the soul of courtesy. He responds to each of the passenger's criticisms tactfully and cordially. The consultant says to himself, "This airline must have a terrific training program in customer service, and I can use this story in my next seminar." When the grumpy man finally leaves and the consultant is face to face with the clerk he says, "I want to compliment you on the way you handled that customer. He was the most unreasonable fellow I've seen in a long time. I'm a management consultant and would like to tell your story in one of my large seminars. May I ask what training your company gives that enables you to control yourself when someone is so obnoxious?"

"We don't get trained in stuff like that," says the clerk, his face expressionless. "They just tell us never to blow up

132

at a customer, so I don't. Of course, that guy is going to Chicago and his bags are going to Singapore."

It is not an uncommon occurrence. There are right ways and wrong ways to give criticism, and unless we can learn to do it right, we will frequently find our way thwarted. The question becomes, then, how can we create a climate in which criticism is a positive move toward excellence rather than the occasion for our bags going to Singapore? Here are some ideas.

1. Build into your agreement with people an understanding that mutual, constructive criticism will be the norm, not the exception.

Some men and women have limited success because they are afraid to criticize and have too great a need to be liked by everyone. So they spend lots of emotional energy suppressing their negative feelings. Then, when the pressure builds to such a level that they blow up in anger, it is so much the exception rather than the rule that everyone panics. On the other hand, if the entire team or family is concerned about quality, and if everyone understands that people in the course of their regular interactions will give some negative reactions to each others' work or behavior, the criticism will be received very differently.

Successful managers hold to rigorous standards and insist that their people produce a superior product. Every time. Hence, they often are perceived as remarkable leaders, when their only genius was that they created an environment where criticism was freely given and freely accepted. Early in his career, Phillip Caponigro was appointed head of a huge sales organization comprised of more than eight hundred employees, stretching from California to Arkansas. I asked how he gets his people to perform so well. "Nothing very complicated," he replied

"I simply refuse to allow my managers *not* to do what they promise they *will* do. We sit down together and set some strong goals—ones they are willing to buy into—then I push them hard to achieve those goals."

Tolerance need not deter us from insisting on excellence. If you are a supervisor or a teacher and never send back inferior work to be redone, your team will get the idea that you don't care about quality. And to have that idea circulating can be disastrous.

The same applies to families. Parents would be derelict in their duty if they did not correct errors or teach the best values and the best ways of doing things. Imagine a master cabinetmaker who never criticized an apprentice, or a music teacher who failed to show a student how to improve the phrasing of a composition. My patients say, "I don't understand why my parents didn't teach me more when I was growing up. I would have resisted at the time, of course, but now, as an adult, I've been embarrassed because I didn't know rules of etiquette, or possess certain other skills I could have learned at home. And I regret they didn't spend more effort pointing out the importance of culture and education. They took a laissez faire attitude toward us, as if all we needed was food and clothing—that we'd somehow grow up on our own."

2. Criticize directly, and in private rather than in public.

Harold Geneen, when he was head of ITT, was famous for the enormous table at which sat dozens of lieutenants for their regular meeting. When someone's numbers for the previous week did not please him, he would dress down the manager before the whole group. Geneen built an empire, but when he left ITT, his abusive management style turned out to have been productive only for the short term.

If you treat people in such a fashion, you do not create teams that can carry on well when you leave. They will eventually send your bags to Singapore.

We are not built to handle censure easily in any circumstance, and certainly not in public. The rule, then, should be to praise in public and criticize in private. Geneen had it wrong: he excoriated people in public and when he praised (which was rare) it was in private.

A corollary is that one should go directly to the offender rather than—or at least before—complaining to others. If you attack people behind their backs, news of your practice spreads rapidly in most organizations and can result in a knife in your own back. The same rule applies for relationships with friends and family. Wise parents do not criticize each other in front of their children or their friends. Nor do they talk negatively about their children when others are present. That is disloyalty.

3. Reconcile yourself to living with human nature as it is.

Certain high achievers can't interact well with others because they have never come to grips with the fallibility of the human animal. Any time you get near to nature, you see that living things are flawed. A flower or a tree, upon close inspection, turns out to be imperfect, and so are human beings. If you cannot take in stride the weak spots in your fellow workers and in the people who live in your house, you will not be very productive. And you will have a hard time finding someone to love.

On the other hand, an acceptance of people's shortcomings will make for a more collegial environment in every circle through which you move. The best work environments and the best friendships are ones where we allow our children to have bad days and bad moods, employees to operate at less than 100% effectiveness when they have distracting problems, and friends to be incapable of affection at certain periods.

4. If you dish it out, be prepared to take it.

It is fascinating to watch those who are able to give and take criticism well. They are never prima donnas, and they work hard at creating a climate where people will tell them the truth.

Bridget R. Shirley, a thirty-two-year-old customer-service supervisor at Johnson Wax, holds informal quarterly reviews with each of the people she oversees. "They appreciate having me tell them things they need to work on rather than letting it slide," she says. "Half of keeping your staff informed is being informed yourself by listening." So, when she gives her staff their regular reviews, Shirley asks people how they want her to improve.

Why are so-called average people sometimes able to create a better climate in their offices than the fast-trackers? Often a part of their secret is that they *are* average. They are open about their limitations and they welcome suggestions for improvement. Their message is: "We're all normal people here, subject to lots of mistakes—including the leader. But we're also a group obsessed with quality and we won't settle for anything less than the best work humanly possible. So don't hold back if you see a way we can make things better."

The bigger your job, the more negative evaluations you must hand out. And the more criticism you must be willing to absorb. Someone has said, "The higher you climb up the ladder the more of your backside is exposed to others, so be prepared for the rocks that will be hurled up at you." The colleagues you have left behind feel understandably jealous and begin sharpening their knives, finding reasons to spread negative stories about you. Those who might benefit from your fall will look for ways to engineer a vote of no confidence. Since your decisions are now more and more public to more and more people, when you make mistakes you must expect criticism from many quarters.

When confronted with their mistakes, some persons' emotions get in the way. They become moody, volatile, or angry. They deny responsibility or try to pin the error on someone else. If, on the other hand, you allow the buck to stop with you and you take overall responsibility for failures—even when they were not your specific errors—your stockholders will respect you and your staff will love you.

I do not wish to be misunderstood here. Great men and women do not shy away from battle, and can be quite vocal in defending themselves. They will take a stand, even if it is unpopular. They are anything but passive, and when it is necessary to fight for their turf or their opinions, they are quite ready to do so. But they are also open to assessments of their leadership, and when they're wrong, they're self-confident and relaxed enough to admit it.

5. Temper your criticism with self-depreciation.

If you are successful and if envy is a natural emotion among your peers or former peers, one of the best ways to defuse their resistance is with laughter. Laughter at yourself. Those who build high morale among their groups cannot be arrogant hot shots who are always boasting of their accomplishments. Rather, they should be candid about their weaknesses, laugh at their foibles, and by such self-depreciation they can draw others to them. Someone has said that happiness, like style, is being without pretense. The person who thinks that the secret of strong leadership is to appear all-powerful and all-knowing badly misunderstands the characteristics of great men and women. A Chinese proverb has it right: "It is my imperfections that endear me to my friends. It is my virtues that annoy them."

One evening a young boy presented a school progress report to his father, saying, "Dad, here's my report card. I'm sure I'll do better next time. I probably deserve to be punished, but first, read this old report card of yours I found in a box in the attic." There is no need for parents to feel they must give the appearance of perfection in order to provide the best models for their children. Quite to the contrary, we make points by describing our failures, thereby showing our children an example of someone who has stumbled, then bounced back. And in the process, we have created a climate in which our criticisms will be accepted much more readily.

6. Counterbalance your negatives with lots of positives.

The famous industrialist of the early twentieth century, Charles Schwab, went overboard when he boasted that he "was lavish with his appreciation and never criticized." But Schwab was correct in his basic assertion. We accomplish much more with positives than with negatives, and Schwab was correct in advising that we be "lavish with appreciation." It is much easier to accept negative evaluations from superiors, parents, and coaches if we believe that they have a basically positive opinion of us and if they outweigh negative critiques with positive critiques. The former football star and TV sports commentator, Fran Tarkington, who now does management seminars, urges that we balance every criticism with at least three compliments. So among graduates of the Tarkington training, it is common to say, after coming down hard on an employee, "Okay, now I owe you three."

The power of positive messages in marriages was recently demonstrated by a group of family researchers at the University of Washington. Most of us in the family therapy field have a difficult time predicting which marriages will fail and which will succeed, but John Gottman, Kim Buehlman, and Lynn Katz interviewed fifty-six couples, all of whom reported their marriages to be happy at the time, but ten of whom were divorced three years later. During the initial interviews, Gottman and his colleagues inquired about many habits the couples used for relating to each other, rated their chances for success, and found that they had predicted which ones would divorce with a startling 94% accuracy. What were the red flags? Among other things, the researchers quizzed the husbands and wives about negative and positive messages in their day-to-day conversations. Fighting did not necessarily indicate a bad marriage, the study found, but how spouses talk about each other and to each other was very telling.

"In couples that stay together," Gottman told one interviewer, "there are many more positive things said than negative ones. But in couples that divorce, there are about one and a half times more negative remarks than positive." At first, this might appear to be merely descriptive, more symptom than cause—the spouses were saying negative things to each other because the marriage was crumbling. But bear in mind that the only couples chosen for the study reported that they were "happily married." It is a much safer conclusion that these attacks were more habitual than the result of something going wrong in the marriage at the time, and that such habits of excessive criticism can erode a good relationship very quickly. Hence, we should try to express every positive feeling that crosses our minds, and when we must be negative, balance it with lots of good strokes.

7. Do not compound the problem by attacking the entire organization or family.

Criticism of a subordinate's or colleague's work is one thing. But if you have criticisms of your company or institution, those should be passed to someone else. The rule is this: *Whenever possible pass positives down and negatives up.* Find someone above—or if that is impossible, at least some senior person at your own level—with whom to ventilate your anger about the larger organization. An individual who is your junior will not be able to cope with those feelings nearly so well. The same applies to families. When talking to your children, beware of using, for dramatic effect, statements like: "We're no family; we're a bunch of dysfunctional people living in the same house." Children do not know how to cope with such general attacks on the system of which they are a part. Except to run away.

8. Assume that people are operating from good motives.

When handing out reprimands it is good to keep in mind the dictum, "People judge others by their behavior, themselves by their motives," because when our employees or friends have erred, they usually are painfully aware of the mistake. But they will cling to the belief that their motives were pure and will want you to believe that as well.

We are not engaging in constructive assessment, we are going for the jugular with remarks like: "I can't imagine what you were thinking. Why were you so stupid?" "You act as if you don't care." "You never seem to try."

Such vitriol is born of frustration and may be justified, but whether we realize it at the time or not, these attacks never improve the situation. They are swords that cut through to the person's basic self-worth. In such confrontations people quickly take you to be the enemy because you appear to have dismissed them as irredeemable and bad to the bone. Even the worst criminals do not regard themselves as all rotten—they believe most of their behavior is well intentioned and justified. So when people think you are attacking their intentions, they will go into a siege mode. They hastily erect a bunker of defense mechanisms and begin denying everything—even to themselves. They will no longer hear anything you say. When two people square off in such fashion, the relationship is in serious difficulty.

9. Object to actions that can be changed.

The other thing wrong with general attacks such as, "Why were you so stupid?" is that the respondent cannot do anything about such facts, even if they are true. On the other hand, if you focus on behavior that can be modified and assume people want to improve their actions, you are on a better footing.

That leads us to the last suggestion:

10. Offer ideas for correcting the problem.

Since it doesn't do any good to talk to someone about defects they can't correct, it will be more productive to point out solvable problems, then offer suggestions on how to remedy the difficulty. You cannot always assume that the other person invites this: hence it is sometimes wise to ask, "Would you like my ideas on how you can untangle this?" (Occasionally, you won't know the solution yourself and must say, when offering the negative comment, "I don't know just how you're going to work this out, but you're a smart person and I have confidence that you'll find a way to do so.")

When John Wooden arrived at UCLA, the basketball team had just ended a 12-13 losing season. He immediately set about building what became the most spectacular record in the collegiate history of the sport—one that has not been matched since Wooden retired in 1975. At that time UCLA had won ten national championships in twelve years.

Coach Wooden and I live near each other, and since we are sometimes speaking at the same meeting, we occasionally find ourselves on an airplane together. I never chat with him without going away uplifted by his genial, upbeat nature. He has strong religious beliefs and is a gentleman in the finest sense of the term.

But did Coach Wooden's gracious manner mean that he handed out nothing but "lavish praise," to use Schwab's phrase? Far from it. He once told me, "My M. A. is in English and before coaching I was a teacher. I *still* regard myself as a teacher and that requires me to correct mistakes constantly."

Two research psychologists once analyzed Wooden's coaching over fifteen practice sessions and found to their surprise that he criticized twice as often as he praised. But his genius was to be found in the nature of his corrective remarks. He would often say, "Do it this way. Don't do it that way. Do it *this* way," as he demonstrated both the proper and the improper methods. Another educational psychologist who studied Wooden's teaching methods called this the ABA system:

A. Show them the way to do it right.

B. Show them how they're doing it wrong.

A. Show them again how to do it right.

I once talked to an actress who had written a successful play. "I couldn't have done it without my fiancé's help," she said. "One of the male characters was very weak at first, and when Mike read it he spotted that and helped me with it a lot."

The obvious affection with which she described his aid intrigued me, so I asked her friend how he had made suggestions with such positive effect.

"Well, first of all, I didn't tell her that the character was 'weak,'" he explained. "When I read it the first time, I was very impressed, and said, 'You've got something powerful here, Blair, and I think I see a way you can make these male characters stronger.' Then I went on to say that I knew she had grown up in a family with no men—her father had died when she was small—and that probably accounted for the trouble she was having.

"The other thing I find about giving feedback," he went on, "is that much of the key is in your reason for giving the feedback. I grew up in religious schools where you were cut down a lot, just for the sake of keeping you in your place, so I'm pretty sensitive to the motives behind people's negative comments. I try to ask myself, 'Am I going to give this criticism to hurt the person, or am I trying to be helpful?' I love Blair a lot and I think she could see I had no desire to put her down. I wanted to be helpful."

PART FOUR
ADAPTABILITY

9

FINDING THE OPPORTUNITIES IN CHANGE

"There'll be only two kinds of managers: the quick and the dead."

—DAVID VICE

THE CENTER FOR CREATIVE LEADERSHIP, IN GREENSBORO, North Carolina, has been studying for some time the reasons certain ambitious, talented people get derailed and fail to make it to the top. In one study, twenty-one such executives were scrutinized—individuals whom everyone expected to go high in the organization but who either flattened out or took early nose dives. The researchers compared these derailed individuals with twenty "arrivers"— those who found their way to the top echelons. At first the two groups looked astonishingly alike. People in both had outstanding strengths, and people in both made some embarrassing mistakes. So it wasn't that the derailed executives made errors and the successful ones did not. However, certain tendencies—what the researchers called "fatal flaws"—cropped up in the failed executives over and over. One of these was "the failure to adapt."

One of the best predictors for success is a person's elasticity. If you dislike innovation and resist change whenever possible, the prospects of success in your career for the twenty-first century will be bleak. Moreover, you will find it virtually impossible to keep your life in balance, because if your world is constantly shifting, juggling your top priorities and keeping them in perspective will require adaptability. It is similar to riding a motorcycle. When you hit new terrain you find new positions and the right speed for the unexpected contours, but the first objective is to maintain your balance in order to move forward.

Seismic Shifts

The terrain we face in the twenty-first century is dramatically new, for we find ourselves in the middle of a once-every-few-centuries revolution. The advent of the Information Revolution may ultimately have greater implications than the Industrial Revolution, and the new era will bring with it both disturbing discontinuities and singular opportunities. We simply will not be able to get away with doing things as we have done them, or even doing them 5% or 10% better.

The environment will shift so rapidly that in both our relationships and our careers we must be quick to seize unexpected openings. Not long ago businesses drew up five-, ten-, even twenty-year plans. No one does that now. Instead of directing an organization or company according to a detailed strategic plan, the forward-looking leaders set only a few clear, overarching goals. Then when an opportunity does arise, they seize it like a striking hawk. An executive coach I know calls this "planful opportunism."

Those in the forefront not only welcome change when it arrives; they hasten its arrival. Certain people win frequently not only because they keep growing within and moving to places where they can learn; they also have a way of stirring up change in any group they join. They are changemakers. A good example is Harry Quadracci, CEO of Quad/Graphics, a $500 million Wisconsin printing company. "We eat change for breakfast," Quadracci says. "Our employees look at change and learning as job security." Quadracci's "think small" concept pushes everyone "to change something, anything, each day. Just start it. Do *something*."

"We eat change for breakfast. Our employees look at change and learning as job security."

Friendships in Flux

Flexibility and accommodation to change are essential qualities for building good personal relationships as well as building good businesses. Samuel Johnson advised that "one should keep one's friendships in repair." Long-term relationships require constant attention and adaptation: you notice ways your friend's needs and interests shift, then, whenever possible, you adjust your course so that you stay closely connected. In my work as a family therapist, I have heard people explain their divorces this way: "Our marriage didn't end with a lot of hard feelings—we simply discovered that we no longer had anything in common. I guess we grew apart."

It is one of the lamest excuses possible for ending a marriage. I wince when I hear it, because my client describes the divergence as if it were something inevitable—as if something in their personalities destined them to fly off in different orbits. But in fact we grow in the directions we choose, and if our mate's or our friend's trajectory is different from ours, it need not be the end of the relationship. It simply calls for some intentional adaptation, and perhaps the sacrifice of some of the freedom and "personal fulfillment" so highly touted among the feel-good psychologists.

A marriage is like an automobile, comprised of many moving parts and several separate systems. With time, all machines require repair. Moving parts need to be replaced with new ones, some of the fixed parts get loose and must be tightened for stability. If, let us say, something has gone wrong with the sex in a marriage, it is a dramatic malfunction and people can be tempted to say to themselves, "We don't even make love anymore. I can't live like this. I guess the marriage is over."

If you are in such circumstances and take such an approach, you may be guilty of what the cognitive psychologists call "catastrophizing the situation," for it is not nearly as hopeless as it may appear. Let us say you and your mate continue to share a passionate love for your children, you both like the home in which you live and the shape of your day-to-day life. Your tastes are similar, you are comfortable with each other's company, you make good partners financially, and you've created many good memories. So in most ways you still have a good machine, with most of the parts in good working order. To call the wrecking yard and have your car towed away because one system is on the blink would be foolish. You simply must make some repairs. You diagnose the problem—sometimes a professional counselor will be necessary, sometimes not—you take the steps that many other couples have used in similar crises, and when the repairs are made, your marriage is on its way again.

Work and Love as Improvisation

When Mary Catherine Bateson married, she was determined to hold to a different set of family standards than that of her parents. Her mother, the anthropologist Margaret Mead, had constructed her life around professional callings and her marriages were secondary. She left two husbands and later was rejected by Mary's father, the psychologist and anthropologist Gregory Bateson.

During her first year in college, Mary married Barkev Kassarjian, who was born in Syria, and whose cultural tradition was Armenian. In the marriage, she adapted. She learned to speak and write Armenian and to cook Armenian food. Both Mary and Barkev became researchers and college professors. His work took them to the Philippines and then to Iran. She did her best to adjust to her husband's work. "I improvised and pieced together a number of different jobs," she writes, "juggling the extra burdens of child care and running a household in a strange environment." When the couple returned to the United States, Bateson's husband urged her to seek a job without restricting her choices to fit his next professional step. "He said that he would accompany me and find a job that would allow us to be together," she writes, so in their next move she took a job as dean at Amherst College and her husband did the accommodating.

Finding fulfilling jobs in the same locale has never been easy for Bateson and Kassarjian. But in their thirty-five years together they have come to see marriage as having many similarities to jazz improvisation, or cooking together: "You combine familiar elements with the unknown, and sometimes you serve as backup and at others you soar free." Bateson has gone on to write several books, among them the exquisite *Composing a Life*. Commenting on the collaboration, she says, "Today it is [my husband] who reads what I write, chapter by chapter, and presses me to set my sights higher and work at the top of my talent." Her sentence is a wonderful description of the dance that goes on in the best marriages, where two people keep adjusting and sensitively responding to the motions of their partner. At times the more supportive role is hers. At other times it is his. And the result is a graceful balance.

Marriage has many similarities to jazz improvisation, or cooking together.

Adaptation and compromise in friendship or marriage does not mean that you must lose your independence, or that you must become more and more alike. But it does mean that you check with each other regularly to notice if you and your partner are tacking in different directions. Then you find a way to change your own course, if possible, and to meet as many of the beloved's needs as possible.

If Innovation Is So Good, Why Do We Resist It?

Adaptation is hard for most of us. We have a knee-jerk resistance to shifts in the status quo that originates in several natural human tendencies. These are important to know, not only for improving our own response time to change but also for understanding the people who work with us or live with us. The better we understand their resistance, the better we can help them cope with the fluctuations we face together.

The Flight or Fight Instinct

Like the animal whose nostrils flare and muscles tighten at a sudden sound, we have primal nerves that tense in the face of quick alteration. It may spell trouble. Our first instinct is not, "Good, we're going to have constructive change." Our first instinct is to panic and run. If recent innovations have turned out badly, we will panic even quicker.

Fear of the Unknown

Dr. Carl Hurley believes the pundits are wrong in saying everyone fears change. "People are not afraid of change," Hurley says; "they like variety. What they're afraid of is the *unknown*." Although it may be boring, the way we're accustomed to operating is at least familiar. The average person has ambivalent feelings about innovation: on the one hand, it is interesting and stimulating, but on the other hand, we find it to be potentially threatening—especially when scant information is available.

Anxiety About Control

Here is another reason we resist any alteration in our lives: we can feel as if we are losing control. Outside forces seem to be turning our world upside down, and we have little to say about it.

The Resistance of an Organization That Discourages Innovation

Institutions, like people, are creatures of habit, and many of us live and work in companies or groups whose philosophy is Business as Usual. When such groups *do* redirect their energies, it is so foreign that it is a huge undertaking.

Success Itself

Strange as it may seem, success can be a serious enemy. One of the most foolish slogans bandied about in management circles a few years ago declared, "If it ain't broke, don't fix it." That philosophy has led to the failure of many companies, because while they continued to operate in the same old fashion—albeit at a profit—a competitor was quietly developing some revolutionary service or product, and suddenly it was too late to catch up. Many talented people who eventually fail do so because certain methods worked well for them early in their lives, and when those methods became outmoded they either did not notice or were too slow to replace them.

The Conservation Impulse

Naturally, we want to protect our assets and status, and one way we do that is to fight off the efforts of people who want to move things around.

Fear That Others Will Learn the New System Faster

It is easy to feel sheepish about being slow on the uptake,

especially as we get older, so we resist the new and the daring for fear of injuring our image.

Taking Advantage of Change

It would be glib to argue that every innovation is for the best. At times we need to put the brakes on change. Moreover, in this period of rapid social upheaval, certain trends are clearly destructive. If you have moral fiber and good judgment, you will develop a skill for distinguishing what needs modifying and what are the bedrock values on which you will not budge.

However, there is a great difference between defending the status quo because we believe it to be worth preserving, and defending it merely because it is easier. When we clash with change, we need to be certain that we are fighting on the basis of principle, not because of the natural inclination to stay in the rut.

Here is a fascinating thing about successful people: they discover, even when their environment becomes worse, that it usually contains opportunities. In economic recessions certain individuals always find a way to prosper—and not just bankruptcy lawyers and psychiatrists. Every negative trend has imbedded in it some opening. For instance, violent crime has frightened everyone in the United States, and we all agree that this is an odious development. Yet those who manufacture, market, install, and service security systems are capitalizing on this trend and in the process rendering an invaluable service. Take another example. Most of our cities' freeway systems are clogged much of the day, forcing businesspeople to inch along in traffic. But those who saw ways to help—with cellular phones, educational audio tapes, and CDs—are profiting from the situation. Traffic congestion also means that people will shop more from their homes, and that opens up a

Could You Make It in Shanghai?

W. Michael Blumenthal was Secretary of Treasury and CEO of UNISYS. In evaluating people, Blumenthal says that he silently asks himself, How would you do in Shanghai?

"I grew up a Jew in Nazi Germany," Blumenthal explains. "I saw my father barely escape with his life from a concentration camp and then immigrate with our family to wartime Shanghai. There I witnessed how people react when they are stripped of all of their possessions and thrust into a totally alien environment. And when I refer to stripping them of all their possessions, I mean not only physical possessions, but of their language, because these were German-speaking people who suddenly found no use for their language or their skills. If you were a lawyer in Germany, it didn't do you much good in wartime Shanghai. If you were a famous journalist in Germany, it meant nothing in China; nobody knew who you were.

"And I have always thought, after observing how people reacted in this environment—both those who were rich and famous and those who were poor and uneducated, and observing that sometimes the latter adjusted much better than the former—that what counts in life is not who you are or where you come from but the inner resources that you bring to bear, first. And secondly, that the trick is not how well you deal with success, but how well you deal with adversity."

multitude of opportunities for merchants to sell by mail or electronic devices.

I once gave a seminar for the branch managers of a large financial services company where the compensation system had been radically revised. The atmosphere at our meeting crackled with hostility because the managers faced a cut in pay. During the coffee break, I talked to one of the vice presidents. "To be candid with you," he said, "I think this new compensation plan stinks, and I'm doing everything I can to get the people at our home office to roll back some of its provisions. I don't blame these managers for their anger. But at the moment this is the way it is, and these men and women really only have three choices.

"One, they can quit and go to work for another company—but if they run from reorganization, they're going to do a lot of moving around. Second, they can stay with the company and moan and complain, banging on the desk during the day and kicking the dog in the evenings. Or third, they can figure out a way to modify the way they do business so this new package works to their advantage. I'll guarantee you that the smart managers at this meeting are already studying the new plan and figuring out a way to make even *more* money when it goes into effect. They don't have to pretend for a moment that they like it. But if they're alert, they'll find a way to use it to their advantage."

Change need not be our enemy. We can, if we choose, embrace the future, and find the opportunities embedded in shifting trends.

If you possess the virtue of flexibility you learn how to use the moving currents around you to your advantage. TV newscaster Tom Brokaw calls this "reading the river." "I grew up on the Missouri River," he writes. "I learned to swim there and I learned to do it in fast currents. So I learned not to fear currents and tides, and I learned how to read a river. . . . What you're doing is coming to an understanding of a force of nature. . . . Sometimes you can't gain on a current no matter how strong you are. Instead, you've got to go with the flow and win on the bias. Take what you can and let the river take a little." This ability to negotiate with the river, Brokaw says, has stood him in good stead at many junctures. "I know better than to pit myself against forces that oppose me. Instead I . . . use them to my own advantage. It may seem like I'm headed hopelessly downstream when I'm actually making progress toward my objective on the other side."

The Randomness of Events

Count Helmuth von Moltke, a nineteenth-century Prussian general, observed that in battle detailed plans usually fail because circumstances inevitably change. A successful strategist, Von Moltke said, must always be willing to adapt. Even broad goals must be elastic, taking into account new events as they occur.

Although they may not know the word, every smart leader understands the concept of "stochastic" shocks—processes driven by random events. When the managers at Hewlett Packard heard the term, they understood its relevance immediately. They had found all too often that they could develop a sensible program only to have it ruined by some capricious turn of events, some unpredictable move by a competitor, or by the economy—that is, a stochastic shock.

In mid-1985, Intel president Andy Grove asked then-CEO Gordon Moore what new leaders would do if the Intel board were to throw both Mr. Grove and Mr. Moore out. Moore answered without hesitation that a new man would get Intel out of the computer-memory business, which the Japanese had entered in a big way and on which Intel was losing millions of dollars at the time.

Grove replied by asking: "Why don't we do it our-selves?" But when he tried to discuss the subject with his colleagues, he says he had trouble getting the words out of his mouth. The whole idea just seemed too farfetched. But Grove eventually led his company to concentrate on micro-processors (the actual guts of the machine). Intel developed the 386 chip, which quickly became the industry standard, and Intel has dominated the chip market since.

Randomness and Relationships

Does the randomness of opportunity show itself in relation-ships? Every day. And taking advantage of stochastic shocks as they occur will help keep your life balanced. You can, for instance, work a lot of hours and still have a rich family life, as long you are watchful for opportunities to catch love on the fly.

Frequently these opportunities occur as interruptions, and often at the most inconvenient of times. Consequently, some of us who live on excessively tight schedules miss out on the best moments of life. When two of my children were very young, I was in graduate school, fiercely trying to stay on a schedule of rising at 4:00 each morning, getting to my basement desk no later than 4:10 a.m., having my devotions first, then studying until 7:10. According to this regimen, I was not to be interrupted until I had logged three full hours, and then I could have a full half hour for breakfast, "relating" to the family from 7:10 to 7:40. Of course, tod-dlers do not understand such schedules, so when Sharon and Alan awakened early, the first place they headed was Daddy's study, where they wanted to crawl up on my lap. But my plan for work did not allow such interruptions, and after giving them a quick hug I told them to trot back upstairs and close the door because Daddy had to work.

Then one day, reading the Gospels, I was struck by the frequency with which men and women interrupted Jesus during his journeys. All manner of persons stopped him:

lepers, fathers worried about their children, people with infirmities, individuals with questions. And he always stopped. No matter how urgent his journey or how large a crowd was awaiting his next lecture, he took time for each person. In fact, almost all of the instances of people being healed by Christ occurred when they caught him on the run.

Looking up from the Bible with a start, I realized how much I had to learn from Christ's example and how foolish it was to miss any chance to play with my children. Thereafter I worked with the basement door open each morning, and some of the best memories of those years are of two sleepy, pajama-clad children in my lap as we read stories and talked until they were ready to pad back upstairs to explore the morning.

That experience is a microcosm of the way love often occurs. The best transactions in families or between friends occur on the fly. They come as stochastic shocks, or serendipities. People often step out onto our path as we are hurrying to a meeting or intent on finishing a project, and it usually turns out that the meeting or the project was inconsequential compared to the chance to get closer to someone we cared for. There are times when we should throw the "to-do" list out the door and take an interlude walking in the woods with someone we love.

One afternoon when Dwight D. Eisenhower was U.S. president, he rose from his chair at a cabinet meeting and declared that he was going out to play catch with his grandson on the White House lawn. When some of the cabinet members objected that they had not yet had opportunity to get to their agendas, Eisenhower said, "Gentlemen, I can explain to you why I am adjourning this meeting. But I could never explain to my grandson why I failed to keep my appointment to play ball with him."

Islands of Stability

One of the best techniques for adjusting to violent upheaval in one area of our lives is to maintain, during that period, stability in as many other areas as possible. We advise our clients who are in the midst of a divorce, for instance, not to change anything else over which they have control. Don't switch jobs, don't rearrange the furniture, don't alter your lifestyle or the way you dress. Try to keep everything as familiar and steady as possible.

One of the ironies of life—sometimes it seems a bitter irony—is that we are asked to adapt to some of the most difficult of exigencies at the stage of life when we have the least natural resiliency: in the seasons of old age.

I have watched a friend, who at this writing is eighty-six, adjust to some of these exigencies, and I can say without equivocation that he is one of the most inspiring men I have ever known. Dr. Lee Kliewer happens to be a clergyman. At age sixty-five, serving as a high-ranking church executive, he was still youthful and vigorous and was asked to stay on until age seventy. During his late sixties, he wanted to hone his skills for the ensuing years, so he enrolled part time in a local school and received an M.A. in marriage, family, and child counseling. "So many ministers in emotional trouble or with family difficulties have always turned to me as confidant," he explained, "and I knew that wouldn't stop when I retired, so I thought I should improve my counseling skills in order to be more helpful. Besides, I have always found psychology to be fascinating."

At age seventy, Dr. Kliewer thought he might have some extra time to tend his garden. (And by garden he meant not only the extensive yards and fountains he had carved into the hillside around his home but also the three miles of trails he maintained with machete and hoe up the undeveloped mountains outside his back gate. "The neighbors and I need a place to hike up there," he explained at a party once, "where we can look over downtown LA and find a little peace.")

But by the time he was released from his job as executive, requests had already piled up on his desk—primarily from churches that needed him to serve as interim pastor. He continued working full time until age eighty.

How did he hold up physically during those years? "Oh, I'm fine," he would report cheerily from some hospital bed if one of us learned he was in for some new surgery and we had tracked him down. "You young guys are busy, and I didn't want to bother you. I'm only in for a few days and the doctors are optimistic." The ailments, according to him, were routine for "an old duffer." Seriously deteriorated hearing, cataracts, detached retinas, cancer. But within days of getting out of the hospital, he would be back at work in full swing.

Eventually the cancer he'd contracted fifteen years earlier caught up with him, and despite numerous hospital surgeries and painful outpatient procedures, he continued to bleed through a tube for most of two years. He always went to the finest doctors he could find, and continued to make two-hour commutes to one of our university teaching hospitals trying to find a solution. The doctors were sympathetic and tried many things, but essentially told him there was nothing more they could do.

One morning this summer, I found myself in the surgical waiting room of a remarkable hospital, the City of Hope, with three other people—Lee's wife, Grace, and Dr. and Mrs. John Chandler, their longtime friends—as we waited out another surgery, this one six hours. What had happened was this: when the university hospital gave up on him, Lee had begun calling around on his own, and with no physician referrals of any kind ("that's how he is," Grace explained as we sat waiting. "He's a tiger, and once he gets on a project, there's no stopping him, so I know enough to get out of the way") he discovered that at the City of Hope, largely built and supported by Jewish philanthropies, doctors had done several hundred pioneering reconstructive operations for cancer patients with his problems, and he had signed up. At first the physicians were reluctant because of Lee's age, and made clear the dangers of such extensive work. Before the operation, he wrote to fellow members of a prayer group of which he was a part: "In instances like this, I'm having the opportunity to see if I really believe what I've preached all these years, and find, without surprise, that I have no fear of death. My life has always been in the Lord's hands, and if He should decide to take me now, that's fine. If I can live for several more years and continue experiencing the good times of retirement, that will be fine too. I actually do feel at peace."

Sitting there in the waiting room as the hours stretched on, I watched those three people chatting and wondered at the affection they had for each other. Dr. Chandler, also a retired clergyman and church executive, turned to me and explained, "My first job out of seminary was working for Lee doing youth work, and in many ways he's been my mentor ever since. Today happens to be our forty-eighth wedding anniversary. Grace sang at our wedding; Lee performed it. We were also in their wedding. We wouldn't want to be anywhere else today."

I looked at the two women with appreciation. Belying their age, both were trim and beautiful, with up-to-date jewelry and hairstyles. I realized how many interconnections these couples had built over the years and how wise and fortunate the four of them were to have maintained such friendships.

When the surgeon met us in a consultation room, he first explained why the operation had gone longer than expected. "The scar tissue caused by the radiation gave us some trouble," he said, "but then that's not atypical." He went on to say that he regarded the procedure as entirely successful and though Dr. Kliewer would have to be in intensive care longer than usual because of his age, the prognosis was good.

Dr. Chandler and I walked out to the parking lot, sharing our relief. "I've known Lee for more than fifty years," he said as we stood beside our cars, "and though he didn't tell me this, I know how his mind works. He was tired of that stupid tube and all the bleeding. He decided he didn't have anything to lose, so he found the one hospital in the country that would try this operation, and now look—he's probably bought himself another ten years!"

Driving down the freeway, I took back to my office two lessons: We are capable of a remarkable resiliency, even in old age. And second, we can handle turbulence and change best when we have islands of stability, like a fifty-year friendship between two couples and a deep personal faith.

10

THE ART OF THE COMEBACK

"The chief job of the educator is to teach people how to fail intelligently."

—CHARLES F. KETTERING

IN EXAMINING THE VIRTUE OF ADAPTABILITY, WE MUST DIS-cuss another type of change—the reversal of fortune that causes us to lose balance entirely and topple over onto the dirt. Anyone who has ever attempted big things has had snafus. Every general loses battles, every batter has slumps, every salesperson has periods when all the big accounts seem to be walking. Moreover, our lives seldom turn out the way we planned. We encounter unexpected roadblocks and dead ends, and often these setbacks are out of our control—no amount of planning could have prevented them. The center no longer holds, and the result is imbalance, a sense of dissociation, and a lack of direction.

By the summer of 1995, Carl Lewis, the eight-time Olympic gold medallist, had hit rock bottom and regarded himself as over the hill. Already thirty-four, with his gray hair now showing, plagued by illnesses, allergies, and injuries for four consecutive years, he hadn't won an impor-tant individual spring title since 1991. In Göteborg, Sweden, that summer, at the World Championships, he pulled a hamstring and returned home thinking he was finished. Sports writer Jill Lieber said in *USA Today*, "His confidence was shaken. His motivation was shot. And his passion for track and field was gone." "Nothing moved me anymore,"

Lewis admits, looking back. "It was a case of been there, done that. . . . When you're young, and you've got a meet to go to, you just go. But, at the end of your career, the fight for the little things, the extra workouts, just isn't there. I'd tell myself, 'You're thirty-four. You've got a full life. You don't need this.'"

But he found he *did* need it one more time. Not long after he returned home from Sweden so ignominiously, Mary Cullen, a Houston friend, had a heart-to-heart talk with him. Her friendship with Lewis dated back to the days when he entered the University of Texas as a freshman. She and her husband Roy had traveled the world to attend each of Lewis's major meets. "Do you want to make the 1996 Olympic team?" she pushed. "I challenge you to make a full commitment. You can't take even a sip of alcohol from now until after the Olympics."

Others swung into action. Tom Tellez, the University of Houston track coach who had coached Lewis for sixteen years, said, "I had to convince Carl he could make the team. I didn't feel he was losing speed. I thought he was losing conditioning and focus."

Lewis officially began his Olympic quest on August 11, 1995, when he began weight training with John Lott, the University of Houston strength and conditioning coach. Lewis had never lifted weights before, but Lott's program was designed to stimulate the fast-twitch muscle fibers necessary to produce explosive power throughout Lewis's body. A vegetarian for almost a decade, Lewis cleansed his body twice through week-long fasts in which he consumed only juices.

In March of 1996, Lewis finished last in a sixty-meter heat and failed to make the final of the Mobil indoor championships in Atlanta. But Tellez told him his mistakes were correctable, that if he stuck to the training program, he'd be ready for the Olympic trials in June. However, when the Olympic trials arrived, he failed to make the U.S. team in the one hundred and two hundred sprints, and it looked as if he would also fail to qualify in the long jump. After two attempts, Lewis was about to be shown the door. Only the top twelve would proceed to the finals after that night and he was in fifteenth place. World record holder Mike Powell, with the day's best jump (26'-11"), had already gone to the showers. Lewis's biggest worry was that he would foul. And it was his last opportunity—probably for the rest of his life. With a rush down the runway, Lewis soared into the air and it seemed he would never come down. His jump of 27'-2½" not only qualified him for the finals but also placed him first among the fifty-two athletes in the trials. He stepped out of the pit and spread his arms wide to the crowd of 81,203. The stadium, on its newly poured foundation, shook from the applause, because everyone loves a comeback. And the next night, Lewis went on to win the gold medal—becoming the first in the history of the modern Games ever to win the event four times, and one of only three to win nine individuals golds. With that he confirmed the old truth that neither failure nor success are final, and he showed us all that after being defeated we can pick ourselves up and go on to win again.

Personal Reversals in the Twenty-first Century

In the new millennium we are certain to confront many disappointments and reversals of fortune. According to a survey conducted by *Fortune*, 86% of the companies questioned had reduced their managerial ranks during the past five years, and most expected the downsizing to continue steadily through the early parts of the twenty-first century. Many rungs on the corporate ladder have simply vanished. How one reacts to a disappointment such as a layoff can reveal the qualities that ultimately lead to success or defeat.

Moreover, if, as the futurists are all saying, the twenty-first century will require increased improvisation, it means that with more innovations will come more flops. So we must be resilient in picking ourselves up, dusting ourselves off, learning from our mistakes, and bouncing back.

Sylvia Erdman's career path shows how important rebound is. "I did OK in school," she says, "but nothing outstanding. Then I got into retailing and discovered I had a certain intuition about customers—a kind of 'street smarts,' about what people like, and that has led to a tremendous career." At forty-two, she joined Revlon as senior director of marketing for European designer fragrances. But after only seven months she was told she was being let go as part of a cutback. The next day was her last. "It was like somebody had punched me in the nose," she says. "I just lost my breath." But a month later a publishing friend asked for advice on selling advertising to the beauty industry. "I realized this wasn't so bad," Erdman says. "People listened to my opinions and said thank you. So I figured I'd keep doing it while job hunting."

Two and a half years later, working out of her apartment, Erdman now has major clients and about the same income she earned at Revlon. She finds the work diverse and likes being her own boss. "I had never thought about being a consultant," she says. "Getting laid off lights a fire under you. It forces you to be creative."

Here are some ideas on adapting to setbacks.

Adaptive technique #1: Recognize the difference between failing and calling yourself a failure.

To say "I have failed four times" is one thing. To say "I am a failure," is quite another. You can say the former and still hold your head high. Anyone in the high-tech fields, for instance, must brace for multiple experiments that result in disappointment. "Outsiders think of Silicon Valley as a success story," writes commentator Mike Malone, "but in truth, it is a graveyard. Failure . . . is Silicon Valley's greatest strength. Every failed product or enterprise is a lesson stored in the collective memory of the country. We not only don't stigmatize failure, sometimes we even admire it. Venture capitalists actually *like* to see a little failure in the résumés of entrepreneurs."

> **"Venture capitalists actually *like* to see a little failure in the résumés of entrepreneurs."**

Everyone in sales must learn to maintain a strong self-image while being rejected all day, but it is not only sales people who must grapple with rejection. Teachers will have students who not only fail to make progress—they will deteriorate. Social workers will have clients who end up in prison. On election night the majority of those running for office will not win; they will lose. When one applies for a job, the odds are that someone else will get it, because for every job there are many applicants. Or consider artists, musicians, actors, and writers who expose themselves every time they perform—a critic can decimate their work, a director can tell them they are not right for the part, a book can fizzle and go out of print, or a play can close after three nights.

But do such failures mean that there is something wrong with you? Of course not. In the first place, the lack of success may not have been your fault at all, and in the second place, if the strikeout *was* your doing, every high achiever has many instances of individual misses. Those who know the art of the rebound have learned that they can be the same person of value whether they are taking a company through bankruptcy or leading an organization turning a huge profit. Successful people are like Václav Havel. He went from playwright to political prisoner to the presidency of Czechoslovakia, to private life, and back to the presidency, all with a certain aplomb and grace by which one can remain the same person in victory and in defeat.

If you are single and date much, you are sure to be rejected at times, no matter how attractive you are. The chemistry may not be right, or the person you are dating may be unreceptive for a thousand different reasons that have nothing to do with you. If you have recently had a string of such rejections, you may conclude that you are undesirable. But such feelings may not be justified. It would be foolish for anyone to assume a lack of worth simply because he or she cannot connect well with everyone. No one can do that.

Of course, at times people *do* seem to reject us for who we are. Perhaps no event makes you feel like a personal failure so much as having an old friendship go bad or having people who once loved you now hate you. This is a far more profound rejection than what actors experience when they fail to get a callback, or what sales reps feel when they get the cold shoulder from a customer. If you have loved your children, for instance, through thick and thin, and they grow up to turn their back on you and tell you that you've done everything wrong, it can break your heart. A business partner whom you once regarded as your best friend can become your adversary in a lawsuit, or someone you helped can bite the hand that fed it.

In studying biographies, I have found several different reactions to such relational disasters. Some pull in and allow their self-confidence to leak out until nothing is left. Sometimes these types spend the rest of their lives apologizing to everyone for everything. Sometimes they withdraw and live as recluses. Sometimes they commit suicide.

In another category are those who use the failed relationship as reason for self-pity. Ours is an age when it is common to feel sorry for ourselves, encouraged at times, I'm afraid, by those of us in the field of psychotherapy. When clients come into our offices reeling from some heartbreaking rejection, it is easy to empathize. And indeed a sympathetic understanding of their pain is often necessary for them to begin to get well. But we do not do our clients any favor by allowing them to get into a deeper and deeper spiral of blaming other people for their unhappiness, or by allowing them to go on for months of therapy talking about how terrible their lot is. The therapist whose only repertoire is sympathy and who is unwilling to get tough (and risk losing a few clients by doing so) should find another line of work. What every patient eventually needs is a coach for the hard work of problem solving.

The people who return to health and go on to rack up future successes after some relational disaster do not withdraw or play the victim. They may be equally heartbroken as the people we discussed earlier, and their tears may flow with equal force. But only for a while. Once they are thinking more clearly, they remind themselves that you expect some ups and downs with the people you care for, and that it is the part of wisdom not to panic too quickly. They remember, perhaps, that this particular relationship has been broken and repaired many times before, and that a string of failures can eventually become an overall success. (One paraphrase of 1 Corinthians 13:7 says "Love never gives up, love keeps trying.")

Forgiveness does not always perform miracles, and if restoration does not occur, balanced people do not allow themselves to stay obsessed with the people who do not like them. They do not repeat over and over the mantra, "After all I've done for that child, how could he turn on me like this?" Instead they focus on the people who *do* like them, and they go on to deepen those friendships. They discover that it is not the end of the world to have enemies. If Jesus could not live without making enemies, perhaps it is presumptuous to expect that we can.

Such healthy persons eventually recognize that a great deal of affection is available out there in the world—both to give and to receive—and they do not allow the collapse of one relationship to snatch from them the joy that will come from future ones.

Perhaps the most common situation to produce self-pity is divorce. When Diane and I met, we were in very similar situations: both coming from unexpected and unwanted divorces, both single parents with two children. I was freshly divorced and reeling from the failure, with little hope for the future. Diane, on the other hand, had been alone for three years. When her husband had left, she was pregnant with Donna, and Scott was one year old. She had no money and little preparation for the job market. The day Donna was born she had no one to take her to the hospital and had to call the paramedics. The fireman who rode in the ambulance felt so sorry for her that when his shift was over he came back to the hospital to sit with her. Later he and his wife brought flowers for her and the baby. At first, the only job Diane could get was as a telephone operator, working split shifts.

But all that had been three years before, and by the time I met her, Diane had made astonishing progress. The children were now three and four, and flourishing. She'd acquired a house and had two college students rooming with her to help make the mortgage payments. Employed now by a busy orthodontist, she had worked her way up and was managing the back office. The day we met, she'd taken the day off to try out her new skis, and was a gorgeous, vibrant woman who was ready to love again. I had to fight off several men to get her to marry me.

All that was twenty-five years ago, and the story has a happy ending. She is now a partner in a highly successful design firm. The children, whom I was able to adopt soon after the wedding, now twenty-nine and thirty, are as upbeat and resilient as their mother.

And as for me? These have been the most productive and the best twenty-five years of my life, and I owe almost all of it to a tough-minded optimist who was dealt some blows she didn't understand and didn't deserve, but which did not leave her embittered: she bounced back like a tree that bends with the winds of a great storm, then regains its balance.

Success in relationships, as in every other area, requires adaptability. Our lives will at times get out of balance, sometimes through our doing, sometimes through no fault of our own. But in neither instance does the loss of equanimity need to be permanent.

Adaptive technique #2: Be unafraid to face your mistakes.

Like all strengths, the ability to handle rejection can become a weakness—we can become so inured to rejection that we become blind to our mistakes. The Greeks called this *hubris*, the Bible called it pride, and such arrogance waits to be undone.

Research on preeminent executives by the Center for Creative Leadership found that virtually all successful people had suffered "hardship experiences," and some were whoppers. They ranged from missed promotions to firings and business failures. The difference between the losers and winners was that the losers were finger-pointers and excuse-makers: they had been betrayed, or the business climate was terrible, or the company was sold. On the other hand, the winners bounced back because they were able to admit their mistakes.

Raymond Johnson, the black entrepreneur and founder of *Ebony* magazine, tells in his book *The Achievers* about a man who was once heir apparent to the president of a large company, then began to fall. "Eventually he gained the reputation of someone who couldn't hold a job, going from one position to another, always terminated for the same reasons," says Johnson. "It was a perfect time for Fulton to reevaluate his personal problems and his career, but he failed to do so."

We have all known those who did the same thing in a string of failed relationships. When things went wrong, they refused to entertain the idea that there might be a pattern or to ask if they might be repeating the same errors. I was once called to see an elderly couple with whom I had worked thirty years before and had not seen since. The wife was bedridden and dying, so I visited them in the home of their son. He had called and said, "Loy, my mother is dying. Please come and see if you can referee this mess. Mom wants to divorce Dad before she dies!"

Driving over, I tried to remember, without success, the nature of our earlier counseling sessions. Their names sounded familiar, but nothing more. However, upon sitting down in the woman's bedroom and listening to her and her husband argue, it all came back to me, *because they were having exactly the same fight, over the same issues, making the same threats to each other, that they'd made in my office thirty years before.* Some of us continue to be frustrated in reaching our goals because we never wake up to the fact that certain patterns of relating are not working.

When an airplane travels toward a destination, it is actually off course most of the time. However, the computers on board are constantly correcting its path, bringing it back into alignment with the destination. Such self-correction is essential for people who are to stay on course over the long flight. They must be able to listen when told by others that they have wandered off course, and they must have the humility to take corrective action.

If you are willing to admit it when you are wrong, that trait alone will cause many people to place their confidence in you, for surprisingly few possess such wisdom. Benjamin Barber, who teaches political science at Rutgers University, said once that he did not divide the world into the weak and the strong, the talented and the not-so-talented. Rather: "I divide the world into learners and non-learners.

There are people who learn, who are open to what happens around them, who listen, who hear the lessons. When they do something stupid, they don't do it again. And when they do something that works a little bit, they do it even better and harder the next time."

Adaptive technique #3: Distinguish between failures due to your errors and failures that call for more effort.

Winners do not confuse self-defeating patterns with the setbacks that call for perseverance. Carrie Sydenstricker was a woman who seemed to be crushed by misfortune again and again. Having gone to China with her missionary husband, she buried one after the other of her three children beneath foreign soil. But she persevered. She bore another child, a child who lived. She gave the girl the names of Pearl and Comfort. We know her as Pearl Buck, who won the Nobel Prize for literature and whose books, such as *The Good Earth*, helped build a bridge of understanding between East and West.

Such tenacity is typical of the resilient people who eventually excel: they are able to endure discouraging results time after time, and still put their hearts into the next attempt. Detours and delays seem to make these people not weaker but tougher. When his play *Waiting for Godot* was a dismal failure, Samuel Beckett was asked how he felt about having a flop on his hands. Beckett, now regarded as one of the preeminent playwrights of the twentieth century, looked at his questioner and replied, "Don't worry about me—I have breathed the vivifying air of failure many times."

> *"I never lost a game; I just ran out of time."*
> —Vince Lombardi

It is possible, of course, to carry perseverance too far. Some of us have had the maxim "Never quit" so drummed into us that we continue to struggle against the wind when we should have tacked long ago and found a different route. Or perhaps a whole new destination.

At motivational seminars, I hear speakers tell stories about some miner who dug a thousand feet into the mountain and finally gave up in despair, then later someone came along who discovered a rich vein of gold awaiting him *just fifty feet farther. If only the first miner would have persevered.* My response sometimes is "Just what is the lesson to be learned? That you keep digging for two thousand feet? A mile? Ten miles?" The time comes when a wise person realizes that the prospects will be improved by starting over in some other place.

Having said that, it is fair to say that for every person who holds on too long there are at least twenty who give up too easily. The annals of achievement are filled with the stories of people whose progress was thwarted many times, but after every defeat they eventually picked themselves up and tried again. Thomas Edison once wrote, "Many of life's failures are people who did not realize how close they were to success when they gave up." If we heed Edison's observation, it does not mean that we will keep working forever on a nonproductive project. But it means that if we err, we err on the side of tenacity, and when one project fails we go on to another with the same perseverance.

"We considered our experiments a failure." The author of those words is a morose man sitting next to his equally melancholy brother on a night train from North Carolina to Dayton, Ohio, in August of 1901. He writes in his journal, "When we looked at the time and money we had expended, and considered the progress made and the distance yet to go, we doubted that we would ever resume our experiments. . . . We considered [them] a failure."

The train is taking Wilbur and Orville Wright back home from Kitty Hawk, where their primitive glider had crashed on every attempt to get it airborne. Wilbur is even more laconic than usual. Once on the train, he rouses himself to declare to Orville that if man ever did fly, "it would not be within our lifetime, not within a thousand years."

So the two brothers return to fixing bicycle chains and patching tires in their little shop on West Third Street. But after a few weeks their depression lifts slightly, dreams of flight reemerge, and the brothers begin to tinker again. The following summer they again visit Kitty Hawk, secretly carrying their glider in "two boxes and a barrel." But when they assemble it on the beach, the high winds whipping across the sand dunes smash the fragile contraption once more.

The following year, their engine-powered glider is ready, and on December 17, 1903, witnessed by four men from the lifesaving station and a boy from Nags Head who braved the cold to watch, the two brothers flipped a coin to see who would try again to pilot the contraption. "After a while, they shook hands," remembered one of the witnesses, "and we couldn't help notice how they held on to each other's hand, sort o' like they hated to let go; like two folks parting who weren't sure they'd ever see each other again." That morning Orville nursed the plane for 120 feet in twelve seconds. At noon, Wilbur began the fourth trial of the day. Passing the 200-foot mark, the *Flyer* was dipping and rising violently, once coming within a foot of the ground, but it kept going and at 300 feet the lifting and falling became less pronounced. On it flew: 500 feet, 600 feet, 700 feet, the bright spread of the wings growing smaller and smaller against the gray background of sand and sky.

That evening at about 6:00, a telegram arrived in Dayton for Bishop Milton Wright, and the cook delivered it upstairs. A few minutes later she heard him coming slowly down. His manner was calm as always but across his bearded face was spread a smile of mingled pleasure and relief. He said quietly, "Well, the boys have made a flight."

11

THE PERPETUAL
LEARNER

"I'd like to grow very old as slowly as possible."

—Irene Mayer Selznick

A few months ago, I sat in a living room in Pacific Palisades, California, with a group of people listening to Dr. Alvin Toeffler, one of the most prescient writers on the twenty-first century. He talked about some of the ideas in his book *Powershifts*. The argument of this book is that knowledge now replaces wealth and physical strength as the primary lever of power. Since the 1970s, Toeffler has been dividing history into three "waves." About ten thousand years ago, says Toeffler, some genius, some Einstein ("probably a woman," he says wryly) revolutionized the world by planting some seeds. Watching the plants grow, the little band of people discovered it to be possible to raise one's own food, and the result was the agrarian age. It was no longer necessary to roam hundreds of miles each year to hunt and gather. People could stay in one spot and build permanent houses.

About ten thousand years later, says Toeffler, a second revolution occurred. The invention of the steam engine opened the door for the Industrial Revolution, or what Toffler calls "The Second Wave." This caused huge shifts in economies and mass dislocations of jobs. The opportunities were no longer on the farm; they were in the cities, where thousands of workers were needed in factories. By the end of the Industrial Revolution, a very small percentage of the population earned a living in agriculture.

Now, as we move into the twenty-first century, says Toeffler, we are entering a third period, which will bring with it similar discontinuities. But it will also bring opportunities as great, or greater, than in the other two shifts. The new age, he says, is the Information Age, and the microchip is to the Information Age what the steam engine was to the Industrial Age. Worldwide, millions of people working in rustbelt industries have found their jobs eliminated, and many other jobs are being shifted to places in the globe where wages are most competitive, with everything linked together via the microchip. But make no mistake about who will get the good jobs, says Toffler: it will be people with the best information. *"The entry card to success in the twenty-first century will be education."*

The good news is that millions of new jobs will be created, more and more work can be performed from our homes, and we will have more and more flexibility in our schedules. From the standpoint of maintaining a balanced life, this can be either good or bad. It can mean that we eliminate many hours of commuting and stay closer to our family and friends for more hours. Or it can mean that some of us will lead increasingly unbalanced lives. With ubiquitous cellular phones and portable devices for retrieving electronic mail, we could find ourselves plugged into the office every day of our vacations, even on some remote mountaintop. Moreover, with the ease of downloading data at home, and with the pressure from downsizing and increased competition, we could find ourselves working more and more evenings and weekends to keep up. The technology of the Information Age can be either a blessing or a curse.

Consider the plight of a Chicago sociologist described by Sue Shellenbarger in the *Wall Street Journal* recently. The wife was in bed reading while she waited for her husband, a physicist, who was working at his computer in another room. She turned and saw him crawling into bed with his laptop.

"It was unbelievable!" the wife says. "You have gone too far this time," she told him angrily. Though he was "thrilled at being able to get into bed with a computer *and* his wife—the two loves of his life," the sociologist says, "I made it clear that one of us had to go."

Despite the threats of these innovations to a well-balanced life, we should not miss the parallels between succeeding in our careers and succeeding in our relationships in this new era. Those who advance at work will be those who keep up with the times and who constantly update their competencies. Those who have rich relationships will be those who are flexible and adaptable, finding new methods and using new devices to stay close to their friends and nurture their families. They will be the best companions for friendship and remain interesting conversationalists at the dinner table because they are perpetual learners, because they are always restless to know more, to understand a new topic, to pile the family into the car and head up the mountains to get a clear view of some lunar eclipse. Such persons are not always easy to live with, but they are never boring.

The way to be interesting is to be interested. You ask questions of the person with whom you are talking. You genuinely like learning the details of their work, understanding the shaping of their lives, listening as they lay out the crucial issues with which they grapple. And in the best relationships, the two of you enjoy learning new things together. You and your friend go to a car show together. You and your mate develop an interest in contemporary sculpture and visit museums and galleries on weekends. You cook together and constantly try new recipes. In other words, you explore the fascinations of the world together.

Studies of high achievers show that they often do not come from affluent homes—in fact a startling number come from families with very limited financial resources. *But more often than not they come from homes where there is a great love of learning.* Books are everywhere in such homes, the television is usually off, tutoring and lessons are offered to children in many fields, and everyone in the family places a higher priority on the furnishing of their minds and the improvement of their competencies than on material possessions. Learning is an extended adventure in which everyone participates.

Knowledge: The Tool for Conquering the Future

Given our rapidly changing business climate, a group of bright people who do not appreciate the importance of constant learning will find themselves left behind. Once again, their very talent will in part be their undoing, for the ease with which they excelled in their early years will have lulled them into thinking that they need not bother with further education. Then, at some midpoint they will discover that they are being passed up by better educated persons. An African-American executive for IBM once explained her method for moving upward: "I went to the best schools that would admit me, then applied to better and better schools, getting as many degrees as I could possibly afford. Then at forty I was through getting degrees, but I wasn't through going to classes, and I certainly wasn't through studying. Anybody, regardless of their lowly beginnings can do what I did. I just wish I knew how to convince kids in the ghetto that education is their ticket out."

> *"If you think education is expensive, try ignorance."*
> —Derek Bok

A Thirst for Information

A psychologist tells about being at the Guthrie Theater in Minneapolis to work with a young cast, and at a party he met a voice coach who had been working with the same group. The conversation turned to Lynn Redgrave, whom my friend had recently seen on the stage in New York. "I just finished working with Lynn Redgrave in New York," the coach said, "and what a difference between her and these kids. Everything I try to teach these actors they resist, but Lynn soaked in everything I said during our sessions, then worked for hours practicing alone each day. What a difference!" It has always been the mark of professionals: they never assume that their field is static or that they have learned everything they need to know.

One need not be brilliant to get a brilliant education. We assume too quickly that only highly intelligent people acquire the best knowledge, but in fact, there are many steady students with average abilities who get good grades and good degrees, regularly take courses that will advance their skills, read voraciously, and are constantly on the prowl for new topics to explore. Life for them is a quest to furnish the mind. Is there a correlation between intelligence and later success? A little. Is there correlation between education and later success? A lot. So the path is rather clear: get as much education as you possibly can, study under everyone you can, and read as much as you can.

No One, Repeat No One, Can Deprive You of a Good Education

If you have not had the advantage of good formal schooling, it does not mean that you cannot richly furnish your mind. History is replete with stories of people who had little formal education, but who became renowned for their erudition.

Abraham Lincoln is perhaps the most obvious American example. The son of an almost illiterate farmer who allowed Abe to attend school only a few weeks here and there—in aggregate less than one year—the young man went on to educate himself. Out of his profound knowledge of the Bible and Shakespeare he crafted, as U.S. president, some of the best letters and speeches in the English language. Lincoln learned early that this took rigorous, intensive concentration. When Lincoln was nineteen, a New Salem neighbor, surveyor Thomas Calhoun, saw that the young man was industrious and offered Lincoln a job. But before he could start work, he had to transform his blank ignorance of surveying into a thorough working knowledge and skill. Many nights schoolmaster Graham's daughter woke at midnight and saw Lincoln and her father by the fire, figuring and explaining. Lincoln's cheeks became sunken and his red eyes bleary. "You're killing yourself," good people told him, and among themselves they whispered that it was too bad, that he was perhaps going mad. But in six weeks' time, Lincoln had mastered his books, the chain, the cirumferentor, and the three horizons, and Thomas Calhoun eventually put him to work on the north end of Sangamon County. This was the first solid accomplishment of Lincoln's career, and he parlayed it into further independent study, eventually becoming a well-to-do Springfield lawyer. That, in turn, opened up more opportunities until he eventually became U.S. president. But he never would have arrived there without his commitment to learning.

Do you want to know how to spot the men and women who are headed for advancement? They will be the ones who capture the bits and pieces of the day that other people waste. Each morning these people on the way up will tear out a few pages of some paperback book, and then you will see them reading those loose pages at the bus stop while everyone else is impatiently looking down the street to be sure to see how the bus pulls up to the curb. They always have the cassette of some book or lecture in their car. They read in airports. And they will be the ones who, upon discovering a word they don't know, look it up in the dictionary, write the definition on a 3x5 card, put it in their purses or pockets and pull the card out frequently to review the definition. Then they try to reinforce their new knowledge by using the word in conversation or in a letter that day. They grab the minutes in order to get more out of the day than others.

James Thurber tells about the playwright George Kauffman who needed to see a doctor. A friend recommended a physician, saying, "You'll like him; he's a great fan of the theater." Kauffman responded, "I don't want a doctor who goes to the theater every night. I want one who stays home reading medical books."

Curiosity May Have Killed the Cat, but It Can Make Money for You

Sometimes the comers of the future can by spotted by inquiring of their hobbies. Those who keep their motivation fresh will not be the ones sitting before a TV screen all weekend watching sports. They will be the ones who are trying to learn everything there is to know about making a mortise and tenon joint, or astronomy, or the manufacture of glass in the nineteenth century. They set themselves the goal of mastering some foreign language. They keep up with the times, they follow new trends in the culture, they are attuned to multinational sweeps of change, and they are always on the lookout for newer and better ways of doing things. They never grow bored, because life is short and there is so much to explore. One of the characteristics of creative people is that they maintain a childlike curiosity. "I have no particular talent," Albert Einstein once said. "I am merely extremely inquisitive." That was an understatement of talent if ever there was one, but his point should not be missed: high achieving, adaptive individuals have an unquenchable thirst for knowledge.

This is not so much a technique as it is an attitude toward truth and a view of the universe. Such persons see the world as the repository of infinite mystery calling out to be investigated and yielding solutions to every vigorous learner.

Because technology is advancing so quickly and information is multiplying so swiftly, it is not easy to keep up, and lazy people excuse their sloth in a multitude of ways. An example. In seminars for a number of years I was telling executives that they should take advantage of computers. The resistance was remarkable, especially among upper-level managers. "Why should I learn to use a computer?" they sputtered. "I pay secretaries to do my typing for me; it's a poor use of my time to learn those machines!" It was a foolish position, for they thought of the computer as a machine, like the fax or copier, when in fact it is the gateway to a whole new world of information.

The future belongs to those who know how to access, analyze, synthesize, and transmit information even more than to those who have their heads crammed with data. And no one can any longer pretend to do these feats without a computer. Those executives who were slow to adapt now realize they had been carrying up the rear-guard and are sheepishly signing up for elementary computer training classes. As Toffler has it, power will go to those who have the most knowledge about knowledge.

In contrast to the big businessmen who thought learning the computer was beneath them, consider the psychiatrist

Dr. Karl Menninger. He was interested in far more than psychiatry. He wrote about religion, penology, and many other topics. In 1989, when Menninger was ninety-three, he enrolled in an elementary computer workshop, and after the first session came back to his office at lunch time, talking excitedly to the clerks about how computers

> **When Menninger was ninety-three, he enrolled in an elementary computer workshop.**

could streamline everyone's work. Kay Bryan, his longtime administrative assistant, says, "Dr. Menninger didn't like not knowing something. He was a marvelous example for all of us to keep learning."

Why Doors Open for Those Who Build a Base of Knowledge

The people who possess this drive to learn often find that their knowledge opens many opportunities. My favorite story to illustrate this is about a young man by the name of Holtz, who grew up scrawny along a crook in the Ohio River—a place where steel mills and potteries erupted black, sooty smoke, and life was hard. He graduated from high school 234th in a class of 278. "Everybody felt so sorry for him," says Joe McNicol, a classmate at St. Aloysius Grammar School and a fellow altar boy. "He was always the last person picked for teams." When "St. Al's" started a football team, Holtz learned every position in order to improve his chances of seeing action.

Later, he went off to Kent State, where he played as a lightweight and little-noticed linebacker. After graduation, he learned his craft as a ubiquitous assistant coach in a succession of schools: University of Iowa, College of William and Mary, University of Connecticut, University of South Carolina, and Ohio State University.

Today, Holtz still has his ears curled under his baseball cap. But by the time he took over the Notre Dame football team in 1986, Lou Holtz had built a broad base of coaching knowledge, and he soon returned the school to the top echelons of college football. During Holtz's ten-year reign, they won a remarkable 76.5% of their games, in large part because he was flexible, kept moving to places where he could learn more, and because he took the time to build a strong knowledge base.

Suggestions on Getting Good Data about Upcoming Change

Successful people and successful companies "treat information as their main strategic advantage, and flexibility as their main strategic weapon," to use Robert Waterman, Jr.'s phrases. "They assume opportunity will keep knocking, but it will knock softly and in unpredictable ways. Their ability is to sense opportunity where others can't, see it where others don't, and act while others hesitate. . . . They behave as informed opportunists."

How do you find good information about these opportunities? Some suggestions:

1. See facts as friendly, even when they contain bad news.

Almost without exception, highly effective people love information. Henry B. Schacht, current CEO of Cummins Engine, quotes his predecessor and mentor, Irwin Miller, as saying, "Even facts that raise alarms are friendly, because they give you clues about how to respond, how to change, how to deal. We have to look at the world the way it is," Schacht emphasizes, "not the way we wish it were. If news is threatening to our current way of life, we *absolutely* want to know it." An executive at Ryder System, Inc., says that

poorly run organizations have the
policy of shooting the messenger
if the news is bad. "Here," he
says, "we shoot the people who
shoot the messengers."

"Here," he says, "we shoot the people who shoot the messengers."

2. Read steadily to keep up with coming trends.

Predictions by the prognosticators must not be taken as gospel, but people such as Tom Peters, Alvin Toffler, Faith Popcorn, and John Naisbitt make a full-time study of new trends, and one of their books should be on your nightstand at all times. But since books are quickly outdated, subscriptions to magazines are also good investments. Periodicals on demographics are important, and everyone, regardless of profession, should read at least one computer magazine every month.

3. Stay in touch with well-informed people.

Some educated people are not readers but learn from those they meet every day. Herbert Simon once gave a talk on information systems for management. "This is the main system," he said, as he reached under the podium and pulled out a telephone. He explained that he stays in contact with about one thousand people. Each of them, in turn, is in touch with at least another five hundred people. Thus, he is only a few phone calls away from a network of five hundred thousand people—and anything he wants to know.

Friendships and the Perpetual Learner

Before leaving this subject of lifelong learning, let's look at one more way the principle applies to improving our relationships and maintaining balance between career and love. In earlier chapters I have said that for friendships, marriages, and parent-child connections to stay healthy, we must adjust to the changing needs of our friends. But here's what often happens: we can get so comfortable in relationships of many years that we stop noticing the changes going on in our loved ones, let alone take corrective steps to adjust to those shifting needs. The best friendships occur as two people make a lifelong study of the other: tenderly and creatively responding to subtle shifts. George Bernard Shaw once wrote, "The only wise man I meet is my tailor. He takes new measurements every time he sees me. Everyone else goes by the old ones."

We cannot assume that we are married to the same person we met ten years ago, or that our friends have remained static. None of us are the same people we were even one year ago. We are always in flux; our dreams and our needs are constantly shifting; and building a happy marriage, like building a strong friendship, requires careful attention to the desires and needs of the beloved then a series of many negotiations and compromises. It is, to use Harriet Lerner's apt figure, a dance in which two people move back and forth, sometimes drawing apart, but always coming back together.

Living Life in Chapters

A friend and his wife, who have made large adjustments in their family life—both geographical and emotional—says that they have learned to think of their lives unfolding in "chapters." It is a valuable concept, for our children pass through stages when they need us present in very different ways. Juggling work and home schedules will require considerable fluctuation as children pass through different periods of growth. In the earliest years, they have enormous needs for our time, and during that chapter we may be unable to invest much in community service. Or if we do, it should be in areas where we can take the children with us.

Unfortunately, that need for time comes at the very stage when many young parents are getting started in their careers and must put great energy into establishing themselves. But for the pre-school years, at least, if there is a way for one of the parents, or alternating parents, or grandparents, to do most of the child care, that is to the good. Whatever delay in career advancement and whatever financial sacrifices are necessary, those will be far outweighed by the advantages of keeping your child in a stable, warm environment.

In later childhood stages, demands will not be as great, but regular family consultations and negotiations are necessary. If both parents are working, one may have to say, "This fall I can't get home early enough in the afternoons to coach your football team, but what would you think if I talked to Tom's dad about taking that over, then I'll be around more in the spring to help with Little League?" Or if the mother isn't free to go camping with the Girl Scout troop, she may be able to compensate by planning a weekend away with her daughter. Such family negotiations give the clear message of your priorities, saying that you are willing to make considerable adjustments in work schedule to keep a balance for everyone. In the process you are teaching them the essential art of compromise.

The adolescent years are another story. Often, those aliens we call teenagers can be cruel. They make it clear that they don't want to be with the family, and it is easy to conclude that if we're not wanted we're not needed. But in this era of substandard education, too much television, crime, drugs, and gangs, it is necessary to be vigilant, to keep boundaries in place, and to do everything possible to keep our teenagers busy in healthy activities. This requires time. They may complain bitterly about our strictness, but all the studies show that despite their complaints, youth feel more secure when they have firm guidelines, consistently enforced. We cannot expect our teenagers to offer much appreciation when we ferry them back and forth to youth meetings, insist that they finish their homework, or restrict their social life. But they will be grateful later.

When our children are experimenting with different personae, trying to determine who they want to be and what they want to do with their lives, they will often need sympathetic support when those experiments get them into trouble or end in rejection. One mother I know told her son tearfully that he didn't seem to appreciate her any longer, at which point he gave her a quick hug and said, "Mom, my friends are important right now, and I know I'm not here much, but when I come home and I need you, I really need you."

The psychiatrist Smiley Blanton showed that he knew a great deal about relationships when he wrote, "To say that love is 'an exchange of psychic energy' is to state a literal fact. The woman who anxiously scans the face of her lover when he is disturbed and reaches out with soothing hand to comfort him is actually transmitting to him a healing force within her own nature. She is obeying the same kind of impulse that directs the heart to pump more blood to a wounded limb."

Blanton's powerful imagery leads us to a final discussion of the transcendence of love in the next chapter, but before discussing why love will still be the greatest thing in the world in the twenty-first century, we must remind ourselves that we can love another well only when we are perpetual learners and perpetual students of the people we care for.

CONCLUSION: WHY LOVE WILL ALWAYS BE THE GREATEST THING IN THE WORLD

"If anything gives us reason to keep going on, it is the prospect of love, that we can bridge the awful loneliness and touch another."

—CARL JUNG

"And now faith, hope, and love abide, these three, and the greatest of these is love."

—1 CORINTHIANS 13:13

SUCCESS IS A VERY RUBBERY WORD AND CAPABLE OF MANY definitions. I have tried to say in this book that success for one person will look quite different from success for another, and both can be valid. The mixture of ingredients may vary a great deal. But I have also tried to say throughout that no matter how much fame or money one can display, a life cannot be called successful unless love is the primary ingredient.

One way to look at this complicated question of the nature of success is to picture yourself at the end of life, looking back. What things will you have done that will have been most gratifying? If you have worked hard and provided for your family, you will doubtless feel good about that. If you have helped build a company and created jobs for people, that will be success. If you have created some things—built a house or a church, painted some pictures, turned a house into a beautiful home, sung in a choir that lifted people's spirits, or maintained a garden that others have enjoyed—that will have been achievement. If you have fed the hungry and helped some people dying of AIDS and visited some people in prison, that will be to your credit. If you have created an environment where some family members were able to help one another and where little children could grow up safe and stimulated and eager to face the future, that, of course, will be to the good.

But let us say that you have done your best as a parent and your adult child is off somewhere on drugs and has not called in years. Does that mean you failed? Or let us say that you and your children continue to carry with them the gashes from a bitter divorce. Or let us say that your career has had many roadblocks and disappointments, that your financial investments have yielded poor returns, that your family has not had as many material trappings as their peers, and that you come to the end of your life without money to leave them (and perhaps not even enough to support yourself to the end). Does that mean that you were not a success?

Obviously it is a complicated question, and you will be disappointed if you have expected to find all the answers in this book. However, on the one most important ingredient for success, I am quite certain: if you have loved passionately and been loved back in similar ways, you will have achieved something profound, regardless of everything else.

In Dante's great epic poem, *The Divine Comedy*, certain virtues had certain positions, but the highest state that could be achieved was Love. In positing the integrated life, there can be no question as to what virtue overrides all the others. "The greatest of these," as St. Paul said, "is love."

And in Jesus' great commandment he describes the successful life as containing three great loves: love of neighbor, love of self, and, above all, love of God.

To function well and to succeed among the stresses of the twenty-first century, it is necessary to keep our lives grounded with a network of affectionate and mutually nurturing relationships. A Swedish study published in the *British Medical Journal* in 1993 looked at 752 men born in the city of Göteborg, then restudied them seven years later, during which time 42 had died. If on the first interview the men reported emotional stress from things like financial troubles, worries about being forced out of a job, involvement in a lawsuit, or a divorce, the death rate was three times greater than for those who said their lives were calm and placid. If they had three or more of these troubles within the year before the exam, the stress was a stronger predictor of death than were medical indicators such as high blood pressure, high concentrations of blood triglycerides, or high serum cholesterol levels.

But (and this is the most remarkable part of the study) among men who said they had a dependable web of intimacy—a wife, close friends, children with whom they were close—*there was no relationship whatsoever* between high stress levels and death rate. As Daniel Goleman summarizes the study, "Having people to turn to and talk with, people who could offer solace, help, and suggestions, protected them from the deadly impact of life's rigors and trauma."

I once knew a man, born illegitimate in Pennsylvania in the 1890s, at a time when our society heaped terrible opprobrium on such children as they grew up. He once told me that he and his mother lived in a small town where it was common knowledge who his father was, but that he did not ever recall having a conversation with the man. As one might expect, he dropped out of school to work, became a hard drinker and something of a barroom brawler. But then he fell in love with a gentle, beautiful young farm girl. They married and soon thereafter became born-again Christians. "I guess a strong simple faith was what a guy like me needed," he once told me, and for the next fifty years he lived that faith powerfully. Moving to Indiana in the Depression, he eventually found a job in a steel mill and spent the rest of his life working there among hard-working, hard-drinking, hard-living men. Though they teased him about being different, they came to respect him for the fact that he never swore, the way he talked quietly about how much his faith meant to him, and the depth of his generosity that caused him to lend them money or help them in many other ways when they were in trouble. Eventually he worked his way up to lead man, then finally became a foreman in the plant. The family had four children, and he and his wife provided a stable environment where there was strong discipline, but where the children also knew unquestionably that they were loved. As one might expect, that love has been transferred to his children's children and their progeny. All four of his children have distinguished themselves. (They are lawyers, engineers, teachers, and one son became superintendent of the steel mill where my friend had worked—fortunately when he was still alive to enjoy his son's accomplishments.)

Through an unusual set of circumstances, I had occasion to observe that man and his family very closely over the course of twenty years, and he became like a father to me. During that time we had some long, quiet talks. He talked to me once about the fact that when he was promoted to foreman at the plant, he found he was in over his head. He simply had not had enough math in school to do the intricate calculations necessary or enough English to write the reports required. "I knew a lot about steel," he told me, smiling, "but I never was a good speller. So, I went to the superintendent one day and told him I'd like my old job back. I said I appreciated the confidence they'd placed in me, and that I'd given it my best, but didn't think I could do the job as adequately as they deserved. He looked at me like I was crazy, because he knew I needed the money, but when I went back to working on the line I was a lot happier. I was where I belonged."

When my friend told me that story, I watched him closely to see if there was a twinge of regret in his eyes. There was not. Here was a man who had not had nearly the educational opportunities he deserved and had grown up embarrassed about other things over which he had no control, but any bitterness about those years had long since been washed away by his faith. He had raised four children in his small, neatly kept house, sent them all to college, and by the time he told me that story, he was basking in the delight of coming to the end of a life into which much love had been packed. A granddaughter told me that one of the things she admired was that he seemed to have no fear of dying: "One day he told me he'd had a good life and was having a lot of fun in retirement, but that he was ready to go to heaven anytime the Lord decided to take him."

I was unable to be at that couple's fiftieth wedding anniversary celebration, but I understand it was a large gathering, with dozens of children, grandchildren, great-grandchildren, and many friends. Was that man a success? An unqualified one. When such faith, integrity, and generosity have been combined in a person's days, the result is a balanced life. Or what Tolstoy called a "magnificent life"— working for the people one loves and loving one's work.